John Bell

RV CAMPING

For beginners

and

CAMPING

COOKBOOK

A Complete Guide with Practical Tips and Tricks to Live Your Dream of RV Lifestyle and Learn Easy and Delicious Recipes to be Enjoyed in Your Camping Trip

Table of Contents

John Bell

RV CAMPING

For beginners

A Complete Guide with Practical Tips and Tricks to Live Your Dream of RV Lifestyle

Introduction

Many people find the idea of RV Camping exciting. It's a great way to experience the great outdoors, have fun with your family, and enjoy the freedom of travel that comes with being on the road full-time.But RV Camping is not all fun and games. There are a few things you need to know before you embark on this adventure.

Your RV is one of the most important parts of your RV Camping experience. Buying a quality RV is a crucial step in getting started as an RV Camper. The key features you should look for in your new RV are:

Preferred pieces of camping gear such as awnings, solar power systems, solar panels, batteries, and other vital gear can add to your overall camping experience.

The easiest way to get started is to stop by our website at RV Camping for the best camping deals on new and used RVs. Our website now offers an incredible selection of new RVs that offer plenty of space for everyone in your family, as well as some of the best new upgrades available on the market today!

Once you've found your dream RV and negotiated the best deal – it's time to start making preparations for your next trip! Now that you have everything you need for your next trip – it's time to get out there! RV Camping has all the essential camping supplies at competitive prices so that you can ensure that each day is filled with fun!

RV camping is a great way to enjoy the great outdoors while getting away from it all. Camping provides travelers with an opportunity to get back to nature and enjoy the simple life without winter weather and cold nights. RV Camping offers a wide variety of camping supplies for those who are looking to head out into the wilderness and get away from it all.

Camping is a popular way to enjoy the great outdoors. Camping in an RV offers you an even more immersive experience.RV camping can give you that sense of relaxation and freedom that you have come to expect from camping. Many RV campers enjoy trips to national parks or other scenic places as well. With the right gear, you can have everything you need to be comfortable on your trip.

RV Camping has various advantages over traditional camping. Many people find it easier to travel with an RV because it is easy to pack and carry around. You won't need to worry about backpacking through difficult terrain, which could damage your gear.

To make sure your next camping trip is enjoyable and memorable, you'll need to get the right RV for the job. Choosing an RV is similar to choosing a new car. Finding the right RV can be a difficult task, but it shouldn't be.

You'll first want to decide whether you want to buy or lease your RV. To figure out which option is right for you, consider these questions:

- What kind of driving will you do?
- How long are your trips?
- How much space do you need?
- What features are important to you?

In addition, consider the ease of setup and break-down and what kind of warranty is offered. Your needs and preferences will determine which category best fits your needs.

Chapter One: Choosing and Setting Up Your Rig

Have you seen a new camp trailer in a neighbor's driveway or a fellow camper at the local campground? Chances are, they could be using one of the RV Camping trailers. Due to RV Camping trailers' quality, they are quickly becoming the favorite among RVers across the country.

RV Camping trailer models are great for camping, comfortable for owners, and easy for others to maneuver. Each RV Camping trailer is made with strong materials and plenty of storage space.

This chapter brings out the equipment you will need to buy. RVs do not come from the factory with anything! You will learn about setting up your utilities, outfitting yourself for inside and outside RV living, making modifications to your rig, and ways to enhance security.

Utilities

Electrical System

Campgrounds are notorious for spikey electricity, and the last thing you need is burned-up electrical equipment or a burned-down RV. In the event of power spikes and sags, the surge suppressor and the line conditioner will ensure you are not a casualty.

The suppressor is an external accessory that plugs into the pedestal, and the RV then plugs into the suppressor. The role of the suppressor is to suppress spikes in voltage, and I do not the $7.99 version found in big-box stores. You will need at least a 30-amp suppressor for truck campers and many travel trailers and a

50-amp suppressor for many travel trailers, 5th wheels, and most motorhomes. These suppressors can be pretty expensive, starting at around $100 and topping out around $300 depending on the features added. Even inexpensive suppressors are now coming with built-in circuit analyzers to detect wiring issues as soon as you hook up and turn on the power.

A line conditioner does two things. First, it serves as a suppressor and a short-term voltage booster. The suppressor takes care of spikes but does nothing for sags (drop in voltage). When power sags, the volts drop, and the amps go up to compensate. The byproduct of increased amperage is heated. Your equipment (especially the air conditioner) will try to compensate and fry itself in the process. It also supplies a temporary voltage boost. Regardless of what you read on the forums, it does not take extra power from the park pedestal to do this. The line conditioner uses internal circuitry and transformers to keep the voltage on hand. The benefit of the line conditioner is that you get two functions in one: suppression and conditioning. If you buy a line conditioner, you will not need to buy an added suppressor. Expect to pay upwards of $500 for a quality line conditioner. Line conditioners come in external or internal versions. External versions plug directly into the pedestal, and the RV plugs into the conditioner. In internal versions, the unit is hard-wired into the RV.

Tip: Bring an extra power cord. Parks do not all locate the power pedestal in the same place. It can be in the back, front, or in-between. That could put you in a position of not having enough cord to reach the pedestal. A 25-foot, 30-amp cord will set you back about $50, and a 50-amp cord can be upwards of $100.

Tip: Buy a couple of dog bone adapters of various amperages (and thereby connections). Dog bone adapters allow you to adapt your RV power connection to a connection of different amperage. For instance, you own a 30-amp rig, and the only power available at the pedestal is a 50-amp receptacle. A 50-amp male to the 30-amp female adapter will allow you to make that connection. Thirty-amp receptacles are the most common power connection, so often they can be loose and worn out. Buy the 50-amp male to 30-amp female adapter first and add others as needed. Also, if your rig is 50-amp, buy a 30-amp male to 50-amp female adapter first.

Note: A 50-amp receptacle carries 25 amps on each leg, so if you adapt your 30-amp RV to this receptacle, you only be tapping into one of the legs, so you will lose 5 amps total.

Solar power allows you to charge your batteries when no power is available. You will need a solar panel, a charge controller, and a means to connect the controller to the battery or batteries.

There are a couple of ways to mount panels. You can mount them directly to the roof of your RV or use portable "suitcase" panels. The advantage of roof-mounted panels is they do not have to be set up as is the case with portable panels. Another advantage is they are always charging, even while you are on your way to your next destination. Lastly, with roof-mounted panels, you do not worry about thieves absconding with them. An advantage of portable panels is they are not parking-spot dependent, meaning you can move them around to catch the sun, even if you are under trees (and your cord is long enough). Portable panels also allow you to move them to other locations to charge other things.

Panels have different ratings, which means different watt-generating capacities—figure spending about $1/watt for your panels.

Next, you will need a controller. The controller regulates the charge to the batteries, so they don't get cooked (especially a problem with deep-cycle, lead-acid batteries). The controllers do this by monitoring battery voltage and supplying only what the battery or needs. Prices range from about $50 to $1,000 depending upon capability and brand.

Batteries vary from RV to RV. Motorhomes use two different types of batteries. The first type is the starting battery. It handles starting the engine and running the motor-vehicle part of the RV. The second type is the house battery that handles running the RV's 12-volt system. Larger motorhomes and diesel-powered motorhomes will carry banks of these batteries. Trailers and truck campers usually carry just one house battery to run their 12-volt systems. If you are going to add solar capability, the first thing you will need to do is replace the house battery. Most RVs come with a 12-volt, marine-grade, deep-cycle house battery. Replace that with 2, 6-volt golf cart (deep-cycle) batteries. These batteries have high capacity and will hold more charge for a longer time—golf cart batteries heavy and expensive, around 60 pounds each and upwards of $200.

Some RVers carry generators. Generators come in very handy if power fails or if you plan to dry camp or boondock. If you buy one, ensure it is an inverter-type generator instead of a contractor generator for two reasons. First, an inverter generator puts out smooth power (sine-wave) for sensitive appliances. Second, it is much quieter than a contractor generator (an all-important consideration for campgrounds that allow generator use during non-quiet hours, usually 8:00 am to 10:00 pm). Generators come in different watt-generating capacities, and most inverter generators have a 15- or 20-amp receptacle in addition to an RV 30-amp receptacle. If you have a 50-amp rig, use your 30-amp male to 50-amp female dogbone adapter.

Motorhomes and upper-crust 5th wheels are usually stocked with a quite powerful generator, often 8.5k up to about 14k (Onan/Cummins are the primary producers). That is because of the components that require more electricity: residential refrigerators, 15K BTU air conditioner(s), hair dryers, microwaves, and coffee makers are the key culprits. The motorhome's onboard generator allows you to run all these items on the go (except the refrigerator can run on propane).

Water

Potable Water Hose: Buy a superior quality NSF-approved water hose in one-half-inch or five-eighths-inch diameters. Consider two lengths of 25-foot hose for hard-to-reach pedestals.

Tip: A five-eighths-inch hose provides more pressure than a one-half-inch hose, which helpsto shower.

Blank Tank Flush Hose: Buy a separate hose for black water tank flushing. Any hose will do; just ensure it is not white, so you don't confuse it with your potable water hose. A black rubber hose is always a good choice because it becomes obvious which is which. Do not store these hoses together and connect the ends when you are not using them.

Water Pressure Regulator: Campground water supplies fluctuate in pressure. If you have a newer RV the water lines can handle up to 100 PSI, but the safest way to go is to plan for 50-60 PSI. Water pressure higher than that can yield a soggy RV. You can choose either a non-adjustable inline pressure regulator or an inline adjustable pressure regulator. The non-adjustable regulator will set you back around $10, and the adjustable will set you back about $75. In either case, it is good insurance.

Another helpful water-related accessory is the Camco Water Bandit. You would use it when you try to hook your hose to a spigot with stripped-out or nonexistent threads (usually at the dump station). Attach one end to the hose via threads, and the other to the source via the hard-rubber adapter. Do not try to use full pressure because it will push the hose off the spigot. Start with a trickle and add pressure until it pops off. Note that valve position, re-attach the hose, and turn the valve to a position just short off the push-off position.

Tip: Keep 2 Water Bandits, one for fresh water and another for black tank rinse. Store them in zip-lock bags.

Sewage

What goes in must come out, and to make that happen, you need sewer hoses. Consider 2, 25-foot sections so you can reach your site's sewer connection, whether it is in front, back, or in between.

You will also need adapters to connect the hoses to the sewer pipe itself and other accessories. Ensure you have a clear elbow on at least one end of the hose so you can see when the tank is empty, especially useful when draining and rinsing the black water tank. Also, consider a clear adapter on the RV side because you can attach your black tank flush hose mentioned in the earlier section directly to the elbow to flush your black tank. Solids left behind in the tank will create unpleasant odors when the RV is closed up (especially in the summer!).

Tip: Buy latex or vinyl gloves to wear anytime you are handling black water hoses, sewer hoses, and their attachments.

CATV/Satellite

Once upon a time, cable television (CATV) reigned supreme in campgrounds, so you will most likely find a CATV input jack somewhere on your RV, either on the outside skin (usually trailers and truck campers) or the utility bay on 5th wheels and motorhomes. Also, you may see a CATV outlet jack, 110-volt receptacle, and corresponding TV mounting bracket on the door side of the RV for those times when you watch TV outside.

A satellite input jack is becoming common on all types of RVs. One jack means that you are going to have to choose whether you use it for entertainment or data. That line is blurred now with the advent of web-based entertainment such as Netflix, Hulu, and others.

If you are going to use your RV's satellite connection, you will need to buy the dish and receiver, and they don't have to come from the same place. The trickiest part of the equation is the antenna. The easiest RV satellite antennas to set up (and the most expensive) are the ones that "set themselves up." The automated GPS unit uses internal circuitry GPS and makes azimuth and altitude changes independently (e.g., Winegard Pathway X2 @ $500). You'll find the highest-end automatic units in motorhomes where the system stays locked on the satellites while you are on the move (e.g., Winegard RoadTrip T4 @ $1,300). Manual units are much less expensive (around $200), and you make the azimuth and altitude changes (each time requiring a new scan).

Cellular Service and Wi-Fi

Cellular Service: Some cellular systems pull in and amplify cellular signals that improve reception. The components are an outside antenna, a power supply, a boost module, and an inside antenna. While sharing these components, manufacturers their products in size and capability. In some cases, the phone must either rest on or be near the inside antenna. (In the case RV systems, the inside antenna is generally good for a 10-foot broadcast range to your phone (e.g., weBoost Drive 4G-X RV @ around $500).

Wi-Fi: A Wi-Fi booster cannot amplify what isn't there; a Wi-Fi booster is just a repeater that receives a campground's Wi-Fi and re-broadcasts it internally. It consists of a wireless router and antenna module mounted on the roof of your RV. It runs on the RV's 12-volt system. To receive boosted Wi-Fi, start your router, then use its software to connect it to the campground's Wi-Fi router. Next, create an internal network from your installed router, and then connect your devices to the router. Wi-Fi download and upload speed depend on the campground gateway's capabilities, what traffic it allows, and how many others connect to it. Just because you have "full" Wi-Fi bars does not mean you will have the same data throughput.

Combination Cell and Wi-Fi Booster: This combines both functions discussed previously into one unit (e.g., Winegard Connect 2.0 WiFi & 4G LTE, around $400 for the unit itself). A combination is a stand-alone unit; you will need a data plan just like a cell phone or cellular service-capable tablet.

Many people build their own systems based upon the components listed above. Some will buy a Pepwave cell receiver/router such as the MAX BR1 Slim @ $300 and build their MIMO antenna. MIMO means multiple-in, multiple-out antennas and connections that 4G uses to achieve its speeds. The beauty of building your own system is you can create a directional antenna, then you use a device to locate the tower and then point the antenna in that direction. A directional MIMO antenna is far more receptive versus the unipolar mount that is the norm in mobile applications.

Chapter Two:RV Supplies

When it comes to supplies, you will load into the RV everything needed for day-to-day living. Think of this as outfitting your RV. Remember, everything you add deducts from the CCC in the case of trailers and truck campers or OCCC in the case of motorhomes.

There isn't a "rule of thumb" to estimate how much weight you should expect to add when outfitting your RV. The best way to achieve the most accuracy is to weigh each thing you add or weigh the RV before and after loading. Do not forget to include the weight of the equipment.

Bedroom: Make sure to load enough bedding to allow for change-outs on longer trips. If you like a particular pillow, buy an extra one and keep it in the RV. Don't forget your CPAP/BiPAP if you use one. By the way, more RVs are coming with 110- and 12-volt receptacles by the bed for this purpose and CPAP/BiPAP manufacturers now offer 12-volt adapters (expect to pay around $100).

Kitchen: When loading cookware, try your best to choose lighter materials and select multitask items to save weight. When it comes to plates, cups, and eating utensils, a lighter is better. If this is your first RV, use big-box finds as a baseline, and don't forget to pack paper products in the event you are conserving water.

A small broom and mop will be helpful, and you may wish to consider a battery-powered stick vacuum. If you are going to load cooking supplies, ensure they can sustain broad swings in temperature and avoid glass containers when possible because they add weight—store food items in rodent-proof containers.

Consider categorizing your cabinets. Manufacturers leave a blank slate, and vertical is the best way to use more space. Use nonslip material to keep contents from shifting. Remove pizza stones and microwave turntables and store them during transit to prevent breakage.

Bathroom: Outfit with duplicates from your house, so you don't have to carry items back and forth. Use single-ply toilet paper only! Two-ply doesn't degrade, and it can clog RV and campground plumbing systems. Consider using vault toilets and shower facilities when available on a longer trip and in a campground without hook-ups. Purchase a black tank treatment such as Camper's Friend and add it to your black tank after draining and flushing it.

Tip: When going number 2, add water to the bowl lay a strip or 2 of toilet paper across the bottom. It makes flushing more efficient and hides the evidence!

Living Area: Add the things you will use in inclement weather (e.g., games, extra blankets, weather radio).

Outdoors

- Animal-proof trash can
- Outdoor carpet
- Outdoor chairs
- Screen room
- Screen shade attachment for RV awning

- Tools to stoke and keep a wood fire

Note: Most states and campgrounds prohibit bringing in your firewood due to the connection between transported insects in wood and deforestation. Some would allow outside firewood if you bought it locally (and you have proof that is). Campgrounds usually have bundled wood for sale at a reasonable cost. A bundle should last an evening unless you like a hot fire!

- Fire Pits: Some campgrounds do not allow wood fires (e.g., Disney World Fort Wilderness), so a propane fire could be a great alternative. Check your campground for prohibitions.
- A coarse bristled brush to clean outdoor shoes, especially when it has been raining. Some people also add shoe hangers to the inside or outside to prevent wearing dirty shoes inside the RV.
- If you have pets, bring dog leads and water bowls
- Bug repellant is necessary. Many campgrounds now prohibit citronella candles because of the open flame.
- Outdoor grills are handy because they limit traffic into the RV, they reduce heat buildup and odors that cooking retains, and they offer more work areas (especially if a table is close by).

Modifications

We Americans are famous for the way we maintain and manicure our suburban yards. We take that cultural quirk with us when we go camping as well. Most RVers start modifying their rigs immediately. It is your space, and it needs to be convenient and aesthetically pleasing to you. Modifications consist of simple paint and posters forthe installation of backup battery systems.

The only limitation is your budget and imagination. The following section presents many of the most common modifications. The best way to discover valuable modifications is to observe campgrounds and note what people are doing to their RVs. They will be a major source of inspiration to you as you begin your modification journey.

One of the most common modifications is paint and wall coverings. Recreational vehicles tend to be dark and monotone inside, with browns and tans throughout. This helps cover dirt and grime, but it also makes it appear dingy and depressing. Many people paint the inside of their RV a lighter color, especially the cabinets. Manufacturers have caught on to this and are now offering lighter-toned walls and cabinets. Suppose you will paint anything on the RV's interior, use latex paint because it will not off-gas like oil-based paints. Avoid nails and screws in the walls because manufacturers do not always frame the unit at 16" on center as contractors do in residential homes. Use adhesive hooks proven to work (3M, for instance).

Most recreational vehicles are equipped with miniblinds that often either break or bend, and it is common to lose the rod that dims them. An alternative is to remove and replace them with custom valance and drapes.

A widespread interior modification is a change in cabinet and storage use. Cabinets are often a blank slate with only minimal compartment separation, which in turn reduces useful storage. Bins, dividers, and stackable containers are the primary means to keep your stuff from moving around.

A helpful modification for outside the RV is using garden hose carry straps to keep your hoses and power cords well-organized. The straps are also very handy when it comes to carrying heavy 30-amp and 50-amp electric cables.

Another common exterior modification has to do with your RV's sewer hose. For years people would store their sewer hose in the back bumper. That solution worked well then, but today's hoses now have tips with bulky connectors that prevent keeping them in the bumper. The hose itself fits, but the connectors do not. There are two solutions for sewer hose storage. The first solution is to ensure you fully rinse the hose and then store it in a large Tupperware-type, covered storage container. You can transport the container in the back of the tow vehicle or one of the RV's storage compartments. Another solution is to mount five-inch PVC fence posts under the rig (motorhomes and trailers) and store the hoses there.

A favorite modification for those who work remotely is removing the RV's booth or dinette and installing a desk. The desk can do double-duty as a dining table. Another option for working road warriors is purchasing a bunkhouse RV and removing the bunks, and converting that space into a workspace. A door separates the bunk rooms from the rest of the coach in some RVs. These are ideal models for office conversion. If you need a larger space, some convert toy hauler garage space into office space.

Arguably, the most discussed modification you will find on RV forums is the original equipment manufacturer (OEM) tire replacement. To hold the cost down, manufacturers install what forum users call "China bombs" (lower-quality tires manufactured in China). RVers call these OEM tires China Bombs because they have a reputation for blowing out well before they are due to be replaced, causing thousands of dollars of damage to the RV. As a preventive measure, many RVers will replace the OEM tires with high-quality tires manufactured in the United States (e.g., Goodyear Endurance, Maxxis 8800, etc.).

Chapter Three: Types Of RV To Consider

There is no single perfect RV out there for everyone. There might be "dream" RVs, but ultimately, the perfect rig is the one that fits you and your lifestyle. Most importantly, the perfect rig is the one that can get you out there to start your adventure finally. It all boils down to how you're planning to spend your days out here. Are you the type that can live comfortably with just a bed and a portable stove? Or do you need showers and toilets built into your rig?

There are tons of different types of RVs out there, and looking at them all can be a bit overwhelming. According to new data, millennials are going to be the future of RV, and major RV makers are taking notice. While retirees are favoring "Class A" motorhomes that can come fully loaded with all the amenities that you can think of in a home, millennials and gen-z's are more apt to choose smaller, more compact vehicles.

The most popular right now for the younger generation are the vans or the class Bs - particularly the Mercedes Sprinter, which has become the de facto symbol of the growing social media culture called the **vanlife**. These vans are more often than not bought second-hand, gutted out, and converted into living spaces. Some conversions are so jaw-dropping that these chic little homes could rival nano flats major cities are infamous for all around the world.

But no worries, you can use this book with our imparted knowledge - which is by no means perfect as we are still learning along the way (aren't we all?) to help you understand and choose which RV best suits you.

First, let's now learn about the different types of RVs. Generally, RVs can be divided into two groups: the motorized and the non-motorized. Motorized RVs have an engine built into the rig so you can drive the whole thing around.

There are three major categories under this group: Class A's, Class B's, and Class C's.

Class A's are the motorized or drivable group's largest rig, and their lengths can reach from 24 to 45ft. A distinguishing feature of Class A is its large windshield that makes them look like a large bus. These rigs come in 2 gas options: the pushers or the diesel-powered ones with the engine at the back - hence the name pusher - or you can opt for the gas-powered ones with the engine up front. As this is one of the largest out of all the available rigs, you can also opt for one with a tag axle; this means an extra third axle is added behind the rig's rear-drive wheel resulting in 2 axles or wheels at the back of the RV. The extra tires increase your rig's carrying capacity and also storage.

On the other hand, Class Bs are generally seen as being on the opposite end of the drivable RV spectrum when it comes to size. Although these are categorized to be the smallest of the drivable RVs out there, we've seen Super Bs that are smaller than some Class Bs. Generally, these are customized vans with an already existing chassis but with the interiors fully converted into living spaces. With their lengths ranging from 17 ft. to 24 ft., their smaller size makes them a favorite among newbies, solo travelers, and people who plan to go off the grid as it boasts ease of driving and better mobility, thus allowing RVers with Class Bs to easily drive into a city.

Class Cs can be seen as a mashup between classes A and B. These have a huge box behind the chassis that allows for bigger, more spacious living quarters. But instead of having a bus-like front, Class Cs have a truck or van upfront. They also tend to have an overhead cab that can double as extra sleeping quarters. Their lengths can go as small as 20 ft to 30 ft. easily.

Class Cs can be further divided into two categories: the Super Bs and the Super Cs. Super Bs often go without an overhead cab and are the shortest, so they tend to look more like a Class B, hence Super B. The defining thing about Super Bs that separates them from Class Bs is that Class Bs are made of a whole van chassis, while Super Bs have a truck or a van upfront merged with a box behind. On the other hand, Super Cs are the largest of all the rigs under Class Cs, but the boxes behind the cabs can go as big as a Class A.

Next in the group are the non-motorized rigs or the towables. These have no motor in them, so you use a truck or any other vehicle to pull it around or tow. Towables can be further divided into 2: these are bumper pulls and fifth wheels.

Differentiated by the type of hitch they go with, bumper pulls are sometimes called tag-along trailers and come in so many varieties it can become dizzying. They can go as small as something that can be pulled by a motorcycle to huge travel trailers that can go up to 40 ft. The most common varieties are tabs or teardrop camper (characterized by their teardrop shape), pop-up campers, and travel trailers (wind resistance is the greatest for these among all the towables, as it can get bigger and also harder to maneuver). There are also hybrids - a mash-up of a pop-up camper and a travel trailer, allowing for more room.

If you plan on getting a bumper pull, the biggest concern you should have is with what kind of vehicle you are going to be using to tow it. Make sure to check and find out how much weight you can actually tow with it.

For the fifth wheels, the difference between this and the bumper pull is that the fifth wheel hitches over the bed of your truck while the bumper pull's tongue hitches over the ball hitch, which is jutting out of your vehicle's rear. Because of this characteristic, as a result, the fifth wheel tends to be taller and bigger than all of the members of the non-motorized category.

And then there are the truck campers - these can't be called motorized with no motor and can't be called towables as they don't have wheels. These campers are sometimes called haulables as they go ON the bed of your truck. These can go as small as ones that can fit snugly in your truck bed to bigger ones with multiple pop-ups and slides that can make them look like a treehouse sometimes.

Factors to Consider

There are just so many choices to choose from, so now, how do you know which one is the perfect rig for you?

If you actually think about it, all RVs are basically made up of the same things - they all have a place for you to sleep, to eat, and to relax while you're traveling. But the difference is that they just have an infinite number of ways on how it's combined, designed, and used. If you think that the most expensive and the biggest rig out there is probably the best, well, as I said before, it depends on how you will use it.

Here are some guidelines and questions to ask yourself that can helpfully narrow down your choices for you.

What's your Budget?

First, what is your budget for all these? It's not just the cost of renting or buying an RV. A lot of newbies get super excited, and they suddenly splurge on the first thing they see, saying it was "love at first sight." But they don't realize how much money you actually need to live and travel in an RV. The best thing you can do is to go below your budget. Around 20% should be enough because something is bound to break down in it, and you are going to fix it whether you're renting it or borrowing it.

Consider every expense that you will meet when you are out here: water, gas, campsites, insurance, roadside assistance, emergencies, maintenance, repairs, tools, your overhead or cost of living, etc. Deduct all those extra expenses and then pick an RV around that range. Don't push yourself to get that gigantic Class A with ovens and a granite countertop. If you already have a perfect vehicle that can tow an RV, then get a towable one - they tend to go cheaper as they don't have motors.

What Are You Going To Do Out Here?

Ask yourself how you are planning to live out here and what you are going to do. Your rig should fit your chosen lifestyle. Do you want to go exploring up unmapped dirt roads? Do you like hiking (up mountains or stream hike)? Are you planning to visit national parks? Do you want to travel by yourself? Or with your whole family?

Suppose you want to go make a pilgrimage to all the national parks and go the adventurous route. In that case, a big rig might not be the one for you - although technically, you can get a Class A and attach a dinghy to it (a dinghy is a smaller vehicle that's towed behind a huge motorhome for easier exploring).

There are various ways on how you can use your RV. Living in an RV doesn't mean you have to move all the time - it's totally fine if you're just planning to park your rig in a campsite somewhere for six months and move for only a few weeks. Or maybe you plan to keep your stick and bricks and just take the RV out for weekend trips? Or maybe you love sports and just want to tailgate? If you are going to live in it for a long time, then a big spacious rig will be more comfortable for you - something like a fifth wheel maybe or a Class A.

But if you really want a big Class A, then you must know it's going to be harder to drive. It's also harder to find campsites because some national park campgrounds are older and smaller, so a really big rig can't fit. Also, another thing to note is that with the longer RVs, you will have problems if you're planning to go up tricky roads and national parks. National parks have length limits. The super long ones that can reach up to 45 ft. long will in no way fit in those roads and campgrounds, but as I said above, if you want and need a Class A, you can always get a dinghy to tow behind you.

What about if you plan to camp out for weeks or months but also want to visit other places nearby without taking your rig? Then a towable might be good for you. You can just leave your rig in the campsite, unhitch, and you can immediately go and take your truck to go into the city to grab some essentials. You can do this with a Class B, too, if you have bikes or a motorcycle with you, but then you'll have to consider storage space issues for Class Bs as they tend to be on the smaller side.

A smaller rig gives you a lot of access to everything. It's easier to maneuver and travel with; plus, you can go anywhere. The downside is that it's small, cramped, and lacks storage space - no matter how many things you build into the walls, you will always be lacking storage space. But if you go big - like Class A 40 ft big - you have all the amenities you can think of, but then the downside is that it's going to be hard to drive or tow around, and you can't explore the great outdoors as much as you'd like with it.

How Long Are You Planning To Live In Your Rig?

This next question is closely related to the second one: how long can you see yourself living in this rig? The question above is on how you will live your life while you are outside your rig.

When you go to RV dealerships or RV shows, even if you are just going to rent it, don't be afraid to ask questions. Imagine yourself actually living in it. I know seeing all these RVs can be overwhelming, so you have to ask yourself: if you are living in it, do you see yourself spending a lot of time on that wrap-around couch with the recliner?

How about that fireplace under the big screen TV? Is kitchen counter space important for you? Do you cook at all, or do you subsist on takeout? Do you really need that 3-burner stove with a full 40L convection oven underneath? Or are you already a master chef when it comes to microwave ovens?

Traveling in your RV and living in it, we think, are two entirely different things. You must find a balance between the two. List down the things you cannot live without and what you won't need or miss, and then stick with the list you have. Better yet - a writer friend had a great tip for this - write down everything you do daily for a month. Analyze what you need and don't need based on that.

For example, you love the great outdoors, so you plan to rent or get a Class B sprinter van with a convertible bed. It might look awesome at first (so cute, so clever!), but you'll find that you'll be leaving it down more often than not as it's such a hassle to make up your bed and put it back up every morning. So, you'd better ask yourself: are you the type of person who makes up their bed every morning after waking up? Not all of us do.

Have you been to a traditional Japanese inn where they roll out the futon at night and store it in the closet every morning? It sounds like a novel idea at first, but stay there for a week, and you'll leave the futon out on the mat every day. You're tired from your adventure, your legs are aching, and you still need to make up your bed. Does that sound appeal at all to you? If it doesn't, you might want to go for a sprinter van that doesn't have a convertible bed.

So check out dealerships and shows, and ask to see the layout. Get a feel for the layouts. Before renting or buying, check to see if you know someone who has an RV parked in their driveways. You can choose to borrow them, or better yet, ask if you can actually live in the RV and stay there for a few days. You don't need to take it out and drive it. Just live there for a few days to get a feel of how you can live in such a tight space. You might come out to gain more insight into what you want in your RV.

How long are you going to own your rig?

This question is for potential buyers, but then you never know after renting one - you might love it so much that you buy one, and then you can get back and read this book again. Is the rig you are planning to get your starter rig, or are you planning to upgrade to a bigger rig after graduating?

Vehicles will depreciate. All RVs depreciate, so even if it's your home, you can't treat it as an investment like you would a stick and brick. Real estate prices can go higher after a few years, especially if you live in a city. Your RV, on the other hand, whether you bought it brand new or not, is going to depreciate in value. Class As and Cs depreciate by around 17 to 18% after just the first year and by 22 to 23% by the time they hit the second year.

Another good thing to ask yourself is this: where are you going to store your camper? Not all RVers will live in it full time, and because storage for RVs can get expensive, that's another expense to add to your budget calculations.

How Long Are You Planning To Drive It?

Next, how long are you going to be driving the RV? How good are you at driving? I'll be honest - we didn't think about this at all when we first started. If you plan on taking long drives to get to your destination, it will be a lot easier to take a smaller rig or pick something that's a bit easier to drive around with because driving a big one is not at all easy. Have you ever had to do a 10-point turn on a single-lane mountain road? Yeah, not fun (especially for me, who owned and learned to drive in a small Toyota). It was absolutely nerve-wracking to transition to something so much bigger than a sedan.

Chapter Four: Towing and Carrying

This section delves into the technical aspects of RVing. You'll learn about capacities and weights, as well as why they're relevant. You'll also discover how to fit an RV to your tow vehicle, tow truck, or truck. Finally, you'll learn how to use a brake controller, set up weight distribution while towing trailers, tow a vehicle behind your motorhome, and remove or minimize trailer sway.

What Are Weights and Capacities, and Why Do They Matter?

Capacities and Weights

There are two Different Vehicle Ratings.

- Curb weight: The weight of a vehicle as it leaves the factory with all options mounted, maximum fluids, and no passengers.
- Payload: The amount of additional weight that a vehicle can bear (passengers and cargo).
- Gross Vehicle Weight (GVW) is the sum of the curb weight and the payload.
- Gross Vehicle Weight Rating: The vehicle's overall permissible weight.
- Combined Gross Weight Rating: The tow vehicle's combined weight and the towed vehicle when they are paired.
- Gross Axle Weight Ratings: The maximum amount of weight that each axle can support. When towing a trailer, this is particularly important to keep in mind.

Weight Limits for RVs

• Dry weight: How much an RV weighs when all options are mounted, and the tanks are empty when it leaves the factory. Notice that some manufacturers include propane tanks and batteries' weight in their calculations, while others do not. To find out what makes up dry weight, talk to your producer.

• Cargo Carrying Capacity: The maximum weight that your trailer or truck camper can transport.

• Cargo Carrying Capacity and Occupant Capacity: The sum of additional weight your motorhome may bear.

• Gross Vehicle Weight Rating (GVWR): The RV's maximum permissible weight.

• Tongue Weight: the percentage of the trailer's weight borne by the tongue (hitch)

Choosing the Right RV

RV (motorhome)

Many RVers treat their vehicles like cars and are unconcerned about their lack of mobility. Many people, however, tow a vehicle behind the motorhome (often referred to as a "toad" or "dinghy").

If you plan to tow a car, make sure your motorhome has the necessary towing capability. Motorhomes with more room can tow bigger dinghies, and diesel motorhomes can tow even bigger dinghies. When it comes to selecting a motorhome-vehicle combination, there are two approaches. First, figure out what kind of vehicle you'll be towing and buy a motorhome accordingly. Second, purchase the motorhome and then a tow vehicle based on the towing capability of the motorhome. Since the motorhome is the more expensive purchase, many RVers buy it first.

The next step is to choose whether you'll tow your dinghy with a dolly, a trailer, or a flat tow (all four wheels are flat to the ground). Towing your vehicle in a trailer needs the most space. Flat towing uses the least amount of your tow vehicle's towing capacity, dolly towing uses more, and towing your vehicle in a trailer requires the most capacity. This is due to the weight of the trailer is added. As you progress from flat to dolly to the tractor, you'll need to pick smaller vehicles to compensate.

Camper Trailers and Trucks

As with the motorhome, there are two schools of thought: buy the trailer based on the tow vehicle's capacities or buy a tow vehicle based on the trailer's weight. The first case is the most typical.

The debate over gasoline vs. diesel fuel among RVers is a contentious one that cannot be resolved simply by weighing the benefits and drawbacks. The decision is often influenced by an intangible factor that pulls you in one direction or the other.

Gasoline: A gasoline-powered vehicle is less costly to purchase, maintain, and repair than a diesel vehicle, is less fussy, and can accommodate more payload capacity than similarly equipped diesel vehicles. It also has less torque, MPG, towing capability, and resale value than similarly equipped diesel models.

Diesel: Compared to similarly equipped gas vehicles, diesel vehicles are more costly to purchase, maintain, and fix, are more finicky, and have a lower payload capacity. Among similarly equipped gas vehicles, it also has more torque, MPG, and towing capability.

Expect the gas engine to work harder if you're flying by the seat of your pants. RV gas engines are designed to rev because revving equals power and torque. When gas engines rev, they become loud, and you'll have to press harder on the gas pedal to maintain the revs in the engine's sweet spot for pulling. Diesel will not work as hard as a gasoline engine, and you will use the gas pedal much less.

There isn't much to choose from when it comes to Class A motorhomes. Gas-powered motorhomes will be smaller, whereas diesel-powered motorhomes will be bigger. Diesel is the only option for dual-axle Class A and Super C motorhomes. Gas-powered Class C, B, and B+ trucks are the most common, except Mercedes-Benz rigs, which are mainly diesel-powered.

Sway and Weight Distribution

Distribution of Weight

The first step in weight distribution is leveling. Since level vehicles hold weight even over all axles, the target is a level trailer connected to a level truck. When a trailer is a tongue high when attached, the tongue weight moves the trailer's weight backward, raising the trailer's propensity to sway. A low tongue trailer pushes weight forward onto the tow vehicle's rear axle when unloading the steer axle. Suspension aids, such as airbags, are one way to level the vehicle. When used in combination with weight distribution, airbags can be very useful.

A trailer's weight is distributed between two points: the axles and the tongue. Trailers are built to bear 85-90 percent of their weight on the axles, with the tongue carrying the remaining 10-15 percent. The hitch serves as a fulcrum between the tow vehicle and the trailer axle(s), transferring the trailer's tongue weight to the tow vehicle's rear axle. The vehicle sags due to the weight shift from the front axle and trailer axles to the tow vehicle's rear axle. Unbalanced tongue weight loads the rear axle of the tow vehicle, unloads the tow vehicle's front axle, and unloads the trailer's rear axle (if a 2-axles unit).

As the front axle unloads, the headlights point up, reducing tire contact with the ground (which reduces steering and stopping ability) and putting additional stress on the rear axle.

When the rear axle of a two-axle trailer unloads, the front axle takes on more weight. This raises the strain on the front axle tires and puts more tension on the front axle and suspension. Increased tire loading can raise pressure and tire temperature, potentially resulting in a blowout due to the increased heat— uneven weight distribution results in unequal braking on both axles.

When a tow vehicle's rear axle is mounted, the payload can exceed the vehicle's capacity, causing extra wear and tear on rear suspension components and resulting in a "squishy" rear end that can cause trailer sway.

The tongue weight is redistributed by a weight transfer hitch (WDH). The aim is to equally distribute the tongue weight of the trailer between the two vehicles' front and rear axles, as well as the trailer's axles.

Spring or trunnion bars are often used in the WDH hitch. The hitch is connected to one end of the bar, which is connected to the trailer's A-frame (the triangular-shaped area in front of the trailer where the propane tanks and battery are mounted). The bars push up on the hitch coupler, preventing the tongue weight from putting downward pressure on the ball. The spring/trunnion bars are indexed to the amount of tongue weight redistribution required: 1,000-pound bars for 1,000 pounds of tongue weight redistribution, and so on. At the time of writing, a WDH will cost anywhere from a few hundred dollars to $3,000. Sway regulation is also used in several of them.

Swaying

You're effectively towing a sail since you're towing a big object with flat sides. Any gust of wind will catch the sail and push it around, just like a weather vane is pushed around by the wind. The wind causes your trailer to shake at its pivot point, the ball. The tow vehicle is pushed in the opposite direction of the wind by trailer sway. When the trailer's sideways motion exceeds the tow vehicle's ability to dampen the sway, it may cause an accident.

Many modern vehicles, especially trucks, have sway control as standard equipment. As sway is observed, the tow vehicle's onboard computer adjusts the suspension and brakes to compensate. When the trailer is attached via the 7-pin connector, the onboard also communicates the trailer's shift.

As the trailer pivots on the ball, sway minimizers use friction to eliminate trailer sway. Sway eliminators project the pivot point from the ball to the rear axle region using a complicated system of several balls, bars, and attachments. Sway minimizers are relatively inexpensive, costing about $75 per hand (it is always best use 2). Sway eliminators (which also have weight distribution) range in price from $1,500 to $3,000.

Chapter Five: The RV Lifestyle's Living Expenses

Anyway, how about we start measuring things? Renting a decent-sized RV from a rental company - anything not too big, not too small - would set you back about $100 per night on average. Now you can start adding up all of the other costs you'll have or charges the company can levy.

Let's begin with the most obvious:

Gasoline. RVs are known as gas guzzlers because they use a lot of gasoline. A typical medium-sized RV will use 80 to 100 gallons of gas every 1,000 miles.

Make A Deposit

Most landlords would need a $500 deposit, which will be refunded if there are no issues during the rental period

Camping Fees

We've talked about camping before, but never about campsites. Don't worry; we'll get to that later. Whether you're going to uncharted territory, boondocking, or dry camping, you'll stop by an RV campground at least once on your journey. These campsites come in a variety of sizes, and they all charge an entrance fee. Depending on the campsite's facilities, prices will range from $5 for no-frills camping to $100 and up per night for more luxurious 5-star campsites with spas and golfing.

Generators fees

Some businesses charge flat rates for their generators, while others do not. Cruise America, the RV rental company, will charge you $3.50 per hour of use, which you can pay after the RV is returned. As a result, aim to keep the use of electrical equipment inside to a minimum.

Mileage fees

Yes, you will be charged by the companies for the number of miles you drive in their RVs. It's not about renting a vehicle from a company that charges you for "unlimited miles." Cruise America, for example, can charge you $0.35 per mile. When you multiply that by a thousand miles, you get $350.

Imposition of taxes

For the RVs you rent, you must pay sales taxes. Per state has its own sales tax, which you would pay in the state where you rented the RV. California, for example, would apply for a 10% sales tax, San Francisco 8.5 percent, and Los Angeles 9.25 percent. So go figure out which state has the lowest fee, and then schedule your trip around that.

Then there are the extras, such as cooking kits, camping essentials, pillows, and bedding, to name a few. These are normally paid separately, so make sure to inquire ahead of time about what kits and other extras are included with your rental. Cleaning fees can be assessed if you return the RV in less than pristine condition than when you arrived.

Insurance is a form of protection.

Yes, insurance is required, particularly if you are renting. RVs are costly, but rental companies and owners want to make sure that someone can cover the costs if anything goes wrong. In any case, you can't avoid having an RV rental insurance policy because it's against the law not to have one.

There are three specific ways to obtain RV insurance policies. You may get them from a specialized RV insurance provider, a leasing company, or as an extension or temporary binder of the existing car insurance company.

As a result, the first thing you can do is contact your current auto insurance provider; some auto insurance plans do cover RV rentals. And if you discover that a particular company covers RV rentals in one state, it can not cover them in another. As you can see, coverage and fees differ greatly depending on the state and the organization's policies.

Then, if your current car insurance covers RV rentals, be sure to ask if it also covers long rentals of more than a month, as some don't. State Farm is an example of a business that covers RV rentals; they have coverage for 30 days without requiring advance notice. RV insurance is also available from USAA.

Another thing to look at is collision coverage. Check with your insurance company to see if it can cover the entire cost of the RV you're renting. If they don't, it's possible that some of them would sell it as an add-on. So, contact your car's insurance firm first and start asking questions to your representative.

However, suppose you live in a busy city and rely on public transportation because you don't own a vehicle. You should use credit cards in this situation because these businesses appreciate it when you use their cards to pay for items. As a courtesy, certain credit cards have damage protection for rental accidents when you pay for the rental fees with the card. These benefits are much more prevalent with travel cards, but even the most popular travel cards do not cover RVs or other high-value vehicles. However, since most cards do not have liability coverage, we do not recommend relying on them for RV insurance. However, if you get a bigger rebate, cashback, or bonus points for using a credit card to pay for the rental fees, it's always worth it.

Essentially, if your existing car insurance policy doesn't protect RV rentals, and you can't find a credit card that provides a good RV insurance policy, you'll have to buy it through or from the renter - which many of you would do. Some of the larger companies will provide you with their insurance plans when you rent an RV from them. They can range from the most basic to the most comprehensive coverage. Obviously, a higher premium would result in lower deductibles and higher thresholds.

Still, most of them (especially peer-to-peer rental sites like Outdoorsy) would simply refer you to an RV-specific insurance provider, such as MBA insurance. Finally, adequate RV insurance will add about $20 a day to your overall rental costs.

As a starting point, the most basic RV rental insurance would only provide you with the state's minimum amount of liability. This will almost certainly be less than the Insurance Information Institute recommends. As a result, it is much easier to raise the premiums in order to stop being underinsured. Paying a little more each day, say $15 to $40, will raise your liability insurance while still increasing your coverage against future injuries and lowering your deductibles.

In addition, if you intend to carry valuable things with you on your trip - which we strongly advise against - your home insurance policy will cover it. But, once again, make sure you're explicit about it. Suppose you are certain you can carry your valuables with you and are concerned that your current home insurance policy will not cover them. In that case, you can buy a travel insurance policy that will cover theft and missing personal items.

Overall, choosing the best auto insurance for you on the road is extremely difficult. Except for truck campers, an RV is essentially a home on wheels. It has many pieces and stuff that can break down or go wrong when you're on the road. It's also a lot more difficult to drive. It will help to know your overall risk tolerance, the kind of RV you'll rent, and what your current car insurance policy covers when deciding what kind of insurance to get for your RV rental.

And it's not just RV insurance that needs to be considered. Good roadside assistance is essential; it may be costly, but it is well worth it and will save you a lot of trouble in the long run. Some auto insurance providers, such as Allstate, provide roadside assistance for RVs. However, others don't, so it's best to check with the current car insurance provider to see if roadside assistance is available for RVs.

If you rent an RV from a large rental company, they'll likely provide 24/7 roadside assistance as part of the insurance package they're giving you. They'll send you a phone number to call if you have a roadside emergency, just like Cruise America. Peer-to-peer rental sites like Outdoorsy and RV share are similar, but it's always a good idea to know what's covered and what isn't. If you're renting from someone that doesn't provide 24/7 roadside assistance, we recommend asking the RV's owner if the vehicle already has a roadside assistance program in place.

The issue with rental companies is that you never know how much wear and tear the RV you're renting has endured. You may not realize the rig is on its last legs until it's too late; that's why testing the engines and the RV before you leave is crucial. However, if you believe the roadside assistance plan given to you is inadequate, you can buy a temporary policy on your rental car.

Roadside Assistance Coverage

Choosing the right roadside assistance for your vehicle also hinges upon your current vehicle insurance provider and also whether you own the RV or you're just renting. Here's a list of good roadside assistance you can consider:

The most popular one on this list, AAA (called "Triple-A") is the American Automobile Association. It's basically an automobile club that offers various coverage levels for their roadside assistance programs, from local short-term coverage to travel coverage plans.

Worth noting, though, is that AAA offers perks like discounts through their affiliations to various hotels, plus rental and repair shops.

Good Sam

Good Sam offers comprehensive coverage for RVs, and their platinum roadside assistance offers to cover rented and borrowed RVs. Also, they don't have distance limits in their policies, so if you plan to go boondocking, then this one is for you.

Paragon Motor Club

Paragon Motor Club's two levels of emergency roadside assistance come into effect any time your vehicle runs into any of these problems: your RV runs out of gas, you're accidentally locked out, your RV won't start, or when you need a tire change. Keep in mind, though, that you will be charged additional fees for any extra services, but it is great for RV rentals as it has a referral program where their existing members can add another person to be covered by the program without incurring any additional cost.

Allstate Insurance

If your vehicle insurance policy is Allstate, then here's some good news: they offer pay-per-use features for your RV. They also have Allstate Motor Club, which will give you roadside assistance and trip interruption coverage. And like AAA, they also have a number of affiliate programs that can offer retail discounts.

The good thing is that you don't have to be an Allstate Insurance policyholder to access their roadside services. For RV rentals, they offer you short-term coverages where they'll just charge you a membership fee.

As you can see, renting an RV is absolutely not cheap. It depends on whether you're just renting this one time or just a couple of times every few years. In a nutshell, it's best to rent only to try it to see if the RV is for you or if you'd only go for trips four times in 10 years or something like that. However, if you will be using it once a year for a few months to a couple of times a year, it will be a lot cheaper to buy a second-hand RV, in the end, every year.

Whether you rent or buy, always remember that there will be expenses incurred along the way. If you buy an RV, you will need to pay for things like maintenance, storage, taxes, insurance, and vehicle registration. And if you decide to rent one, as stated above, be prepared to shell out a lot of money for the extras, mileage fees, campsites and generator fees, and insurance. As I said above, whatever budget you set aside for this, it's always better to 20% lower. Time to whip out those Excel spreadsheets and start budgeting!

Chapter Six: Planning Your RV Trips

Where to Captain?

It is necessary to decide where and why you want to visit, especially for beginners to the world of RV. This chapter will help you choose a place that will be best for you.

Where Do You Want to Travel?

The first thing to choose is what sort of places you want to travel to. Do you want to explore bigger cities or do you want to visit remote places etc.? The place you want to visit will affect many decisions, the foremost being what sort of vehicle you need to buy. For instance, if you plan to visit big cities, you should buy a small trailer instead of a bigger machine. If you want to visit open roads, then investing in a bigger setup is a viable option. You should also check the places' rules and regulations, as certain places do not allow bigger vehicles.

How Do You Want to Travel?

Many people do not realize that people like to travel in different ways. If you are more interested in enjoying the outside world, it is recommended to choose a smaller vehicle. If you want to enjoy all the comforts of your home while living outside, then investing in a bigger option will be better.

How Much Space Do You Need?

This question cannot be answered until you get out on the road. Some people think that they can handle living in a small setup; however, they soon realize that they need a bigger place once they hit the road. To help you make this decision, consult with expert RV campers and RV superstores. These people can help you have a vision of what sort of setup will be the best for you.

How Much Can You Spend?

Another thing that you need to consider while choosing a suitable place is how much you can spend. This is an individualistic option, and everyone's budget as well as will to pay is different. Do not visit a place that is out of your budget.

How Comfortable Are You Pulling a Camper?

Adjusting to the RV life takes some time, and learning how to maneuver one takes time as well. Whether your vehicle is small or large, it will take time to learn how to drive, park, and back it up. If you do not feel comfortable about driving it on your own, it is recommended to join an RV school that can help you learn how to drive one carefully. This is essential for people who want to visit places that are considered to be risky.

Where to Camp in Your RV

When you hear the word RV, what is the first image that comes to your mind? Is it spending a dream week at a peaceful, serene, and solitary campsite? Or is it a fun, busy RV park with new friends and fascinating conversations around campfires? The images might be different; however, an RV camping trip's main aspect is always to enjoy and have fun. RV camping has something for everyone if you know how to find it.

There are numerous camping options available for every budget; for instance, some options such as RV resorts can be quite expensive; however, certain other options such as boondocking are free.

Let us look at some of the most common camping sites and why you should choose them.

RV Parks

RV parks are one of the most popular sites for camping. These are privately owned campgrounds that are specifically designed for RV campers. RV parks offer either partial or full hookups. Full hookups allow you to enjoy unlimited electricity, water, and sewage services. In partial hookups, everything is available except sewage services.

RV parks are easily accessible. You can easily get in and get out of these parks, as they are located near major highways. Many RV parks also offer other services such as free Wi-Fi and on-site laundry. RV parks popular with families also offer planned activities for children, game rooms, hiking trails, mini-golf, horse rides, pool, kayaking, and other related activities.

While RV parks are a great way to enjoy your holiday without forgoing the comforts and pleasure, not everyone loves them. RV parks are often crowded throughout the year, and they are especially crowded in summers. Parks that are located near crowded cities are often packed during the vacation season. There is often very little place between two rigs, and it may feel too congested to many.

How to Find RV Parks

Finding an RV park and reserving it is quite simple, as many services and websites can help you do so. Reserve America is a great service through which you can find an RV park and reserve a place as well. It is recommended to check the reviews of the park before reserving it on RV Park Reviews.

For frequent campers, buying the AllStays app can be a great decision. It is available for $9.99, and every cent is worth it. You can find all kinds of campsites through this app, right from state rec areas to RV parks and even boondocking places. It also features other relevant information such as incline and elevation of the campsite, reviews of grounds, different amenities, etc.

You can also find out about RV parks by joining various clubs such as Good Sam, Escapees, Passport America, etc. These clubs have annual membership fees; however, through these memberships, you will be able to score huge discounts on various campgrounds throughout the nation.

State and National Parks

Public parks are a great option for camping. These places are good for people who love solitude, natural beauty, and silence. If you desire to relax and get away from the hustle and bustle of urban life, you should definitely camp at a national or state park.

Finding a National or State Park

Finding a national park is quite easy as all national parks are listed on the National Park Service's website. Do remember that you cannot stay at a national park unless you have made a reservation.

Costs

The price of staying at a National park varies according to the park, the campgrounds, and the amenities. It has been observed that prices may vary between campgrounds even if they are in the same park. For instance, the Great Smokey Mountain National Park has many campgrounds ranging from $14 to $23 per night.

If you are a frequent traveler and want to visit many national parks throughout the nation, then it is recommended to get the $80 Annual Pass. This will cover entrance fees to all the parks. If you are 62 years and older, you can buy this pass for $10. Seniors also enjoy a 50% (up to) discount on camping fees. If you are a US military member or are a dependent US military member, you are qualified to get an Annual Pass.

The costs of state parks vary according to states, duration, the period of camping, etc. For instance, if you visit a state park during the peak camping season, then you may have to pay $20 to $45 for an excellent campsite at a popular park. You may also have to pay a reservation fee that may go up to $9.

How to Act at Retail Locations

Many retail locations provide free overnight staying opportunities in the form of boondocking; however, you need to follow a code of conduct while staying at such places. Always ask the store manager whether it is allowed to stay at their store overnight. Do not park unless they allow you to do so. Almost all stores are open to people camping in their parking lots. Some stores do not allow you to do so due to the cities' rules and regulations or towns they are situated in. It is always better and polite to ask for permission.

Always be discreet and respect others' space. Do not put out lawn chairs and start drinking. Stores allow people to park overnight as a courteous move; it is therefore recommended to keep it quiet and peaceful. You can repay the courtesy by shopping at the store and cleaning after you every time you leave a place.

Useful RV Trip Planning Apps

Smartphones are important for travelers as they let us keep in touch with our loved ones; however, smartphones are much more than just connecting devices, and you can use them to make your trips extremely easy and restful as well. Here are some RV apps that you can use to make your RV experience smooth and delightful.

Yelp

Good old Yelp is a great service to check out reviews of various things and services. You will be surprised to know that it has more than 50 million reviews written by customers worldwide. Yelp was primarily concerned with food-based services and locations such as restaurants, take-outs, hotels, dinners, etc. now, Yelp has expanded its service to cater to various other locations. It is a wonderful app to find the best places near you.

AllTrails

This app gives the best choice to people who love nature and love to be outside. This app features over 50,000 trails and hikes all across North America. The information about these trails is not basic and is rich with pictures, tracks, reviews, etc. It also contains information about outdoor activities, including fly-fishing, hiking, biking, etc. The app is GPS enabled so you can either find the closest trail next to you, or you can also input data and find a trail in the nearby state. You can also track your activity to make a new trail and post it on the app to use others.

GasBuddy

One of the main aspects of an RV trip is gas money. Often people go over budget because they do not plan their gas buying strategies properly. GasBuddy will help you find the cheapest gas stations near you. You can also search for gas stations using postal codes and cities. It is GPS enabled, and with a simple click, you can find the best gas place near you. If you find a gas station that is not available on the app, you can post it and earn award points. The app is currently available for Canada and the USA.

WiFi Map

Through this app, you can check the free Wi-Fi throughout the world along with their passwords. This app works offline as well, and you can type in your location and find good Wi-Fi close to you. It is a must-have app for everyone who travels often and who likes to be connected all the time.

RV Parky

Through this app, you will be able to find more than 25,000 campgrounds, parks, Walmarts, rest areas, campgrounds, etc., throughout the nation. You will also be able to check out the reviews and pictures of the places. It is a must-have app for every RV enthusiast.

Passport America

Passport America is an old service offering 50% discounts on camping clubs since the year 1992. Now it offers more than 1800 locations throughout Mexico, Canada as well as the USA. It is now free to download for members and non-members who want to browse through the list of RV Parks, Campgrounds, Resorts, etc.

SatFinder

This tool is essential if you want to set up your satellite dish, as it will help you by pointing towards the strongest signal according to your GPS location.

Sandidumps RV Dump Station

This app will allow you to find dump stations all over the Internet while you are driving. It is GPS enabled, so it will help you find the closest station with ease. If you plan to visit some other city, you can also manually enter the city and locate dump spots.

Instagram

Instagram is one of the best photo-sharing social media apps. It's an amazing platform to document your photographs and your journey. It will help you share your photos with your friends, families, and even strangers. It is a great way to keep your life and moments of fun in a well-documented format.

Roadtrippers

While there exist many paid options for RV road planners, Roadtrippers is a great free alternative that is still potent and feature-rich. It will solve all your problems. It will help discover the best viewing and scenic spots, best eateries, hotels, rest houses, attractions, and many more. You will be able to plan a new trip right from your app, or you can also plan one on the app's website roadtrippers.com and then sync it to your app.

Overnight Parking Finder (Android)

This app is available on the Android platform. Through this app, you will find many free overnight parking spots in a nearby Walmart. It also has a turn-by-turn guiding system and a RedBox locator that can help you locate every RedBox in the USA.

Weather Bug

Weather is an essential aspect if you want your camping trip to be comfortable and fun. Through this app, you will be able to keep a close eye on weather changes and receive almost instant alerts. It has a special Spark lighting alert that will calculate the distance of lighting. It will also help you save energy costs as it features a home energy meter.

Key Ring

With this app's help, you will never have to carry a membership card or a loyalty card anymore. This app will keep everything in one place. This includes shopping lists, rewards, coupons, weekly ads, loyalty cards, etc.

RV Checklist

It is a great app for everyone who owns an RV and is forgetful. It will allow you to be well prepared for your trips and make sure that you do not forget anything important. It will also keep an eye on your progress related to important tasks. You can make different lists according to your need.

Chapter Seven: RVers' Top Destinations

People often purchase new RVs and become excited about traveling, only to spend a lot of time and money in boring and uninteresting locations. Experienced travelers should be listened to, and hyped places should be avoided. Only by doing so would you be able to locate the ideal locations. Let's take a look at three of the most common RV destinations perfect for everyone in this segment.

Before going on an RV tour, one of the most important things to remember is where you live. Aside from that, you must consider your budget and time constraints. These factors will assist you in deciding where you want to go. A lot of preparation is required to make a trip successful, particularly if you are a beginner. Few people in the world can pull off an impromptu RV ride. A well-planned trip would ensure a healthy and enjoyable experience.

Seasons and the environment are also important considerations to consider before deciding on a destination. An RV ride is essentially a long road trip. If you like crowded areas and the hustle and bustle, it is best to avoid tourist traps and major cities. These establishments are, however, very pricey. Here is a small list of top RV destinations in the United States if you, like most RVers, want to visit a serene, quiet, and scenic location.

Yellowstone National Park

Yellowstone National Park's journey is as breathtaking as the park itself. Along the way, you can stop by the Bighorn National Recreation Area and Devil's Tower National Monument, which are both breathtaking. If the weather permits, you can also visit the

Beartooth Pass, which offers spectacular views of the Grand Tetons and other mountain ranges surrounding Yellowstone.

Often try to arrive at the campsite early in the morning to ensure that you get a good spot. Yellowstone is a large and beautiful park, but it has few amenities and campgrounds. As a result, it is advised that you arrive early to secure the best spot.

You should certainly go to Old Faithful, which is considered the Yellowstone Grand Canyon. Paint Pots and the geyser basin are also worth seeing. Yellowstone is the perfect spot to go fishing if you like it. Although hiking is a great way to see the park's beauty, it is recommended that you keep an eye out for as many wild bears as possible.

If you aren't familiar with trip planning, Yellowstone could be very expensive. It is recommended that you work with an experienced RVer who can help you make sound and cost-effective plans.

You would not want to leave Yellowstone until you have seen its tranquility, beauty, and delight.

The South Dakota Black Hills

The Black Hills of South Dakota is a popular destination for RVers from all over the country because they offer a stunning natural setting and a range of activities and events.

Setting up a base camp in the hills is suggested before visiting the Badlands National Park and the Wall Drug. The Rapid City and Sioux museums are both worth seeing.

Custer State Park offers wildlife, stunning scenery, games, and fun if you have enough time. Custer State Park offers a variety of events for all members of the family to enjoy. Hiking trails, campgrounds, museums, and other attractions are all available.

Spend some time in Lead and Deadwood, as well. Two small mining towns have survived due to thriving casino industry. If you have enough time to visit the Pine Ridge Indian Reservation, you will see old gold mines, cemeteries, museums, and so on. You might be able to attend a Native American Powwow if you're lucky.

Mount Rushmore and the Mad Horse Memorial are both worth seeing. You will be able to see the annual Sturgis motorcycle rally if you visit in early August.

Ten campgrounds, four lodges, four fishing lakes, six hiking trails, two small museums, and a summer theatre are available at Custer State Park. There is also a small church there.

You can also go gold panning, hiking, and attending a barn dance. The Black Hills are ideal for first-time RVers.

Biloxi, Mississippi

Biloxi is a small town in Mississippi, close to the Florida border. Since it has so many stunning and thrilling casinos, many people consider it a smaller Las Vegas version. It also has antique stores, white sand beaches, and delicious seafood. In comparison to beaches on the west coast, the beaches in this area are clean and much less crowded.

Biloxi is also known for being a military town, so if you happen to be in the region around July 4th, you're in for a treat. You can see a degree of patriotism and love for the country that is unmatched elsewhere in the United States. You can camp for free in this town if you have a National Park Pass. You can choose to remain near the Gulf Island National Seashore, just five miles from the casinos. The place is inexpensive, and you will not go over your budget.

People flock to Biloxi because the casino is fun, the food is delicious, and there are a variety of clubs to join.

While Hurricane Katrina caused some damage to Biloxi, it has since been rebuilt and restored to its former glory. You can also pay a visit to the town's Katrina memorial.

It's a beautiful and interesting city to visit, and it'll be well worth your time.

10 Things to Know When RVing in Canada

Canada is a wonderful place for RVers as it is extremely friendly, beautiful, and culturally rich. It is also incredibly safe, and your trip will almost always go without a hitch if you take certain things into account and keep certain things in mind while visiting. Here is a small list of things that you need to consider before visiting Canada with an RV.

1. Border Crossings

Canada and the US have an international boundary maintained by US Customs and Border Protection on the south and CBSA or Canada Border Services on the north. It is a simple border, and you can cross it in a couple of minutes. You need to be prepared in advance if you want to make this border crossing smooth and bump-free.

Important items to prepare when entering Canada from the United States:

Identification: While a passport is the best form of ID, you should also carry a citizenship certificate, a birth certificate, a U.S. Permanent Resident with a photo, etc.

Children and Pets: You can cross the border with ease even if you have children with you; however, if one or both custodial parents of the children aren't with you, you must procure and provide a consent letter. You can travel with a pet with ease if you have the necessary documents with you. The Canadian Food Inspection Agency manages pet and pet travel.

Food and Alcohol: It is recommended to contact CBSA to check the current restrictions as laws change frequently. There are certain rules and regulations about how much alcohol and tobacco you carry while crossing the border for free. After a certain amount, you will have to pay for these two substances.

Gun Laws: While it is okay to carry guns in Canada, it is not as gun-friendly as the USA. You can carry guns in Canada by contacting the CBSA, and you will need to do some paperwork before you bring along your trusty friend.

2. Monetary System / Banking

Sometimes Canadian money is called 'funny money because it is very colorful and vibrant. It is also waterproof and is made of a special kind of plastic. Two coins called Loonie and Toonie are used instead of one and two dollar bills. Pennies are not used in Canada.

While US dollars are accepted almost everywhere, they are often taken at par. This means they are considered to be equivalent to Canadian dollars. This may incur a loss, as the US currency is higher than the Canadian currency. The best way to avoid losses is by using debit or credit cards to get each day's exchange rate.

ATMs and bank outlets are present everywhere and are simple to use; however, you may need to pay a small fee to use the devices. This fee varies according to the place and time. Canadians use debit cards a lot, so almost all retail stores and outlets will accept them.

While credit cards are popular, too, it is recommended to contact your bank and inform them that you are traveling out of the nation so that they won't block your account thinking it was stolen.

3. Driving

You need to carry proof of auto insurance as well as a valid and current driver's license if you want to drive in Canada. US licenses and insurance papers are accepted in Canada, so you do not need to get new ones.

It is recommended to keep a close eye on the speed limit especially if you are not used to the metric system. You may get confused and cross the speed limit, which may result in a big fine.

There are central laws that are implemented throughout the nation; however, there are certain region-specific rules. Do not talk on the phone while driving, or you will incur a huge fine. You may talk on the phone if it is in hands-free mode.

Seatbelts are extremely important in Canada, and you need to wear seatbelts all the time. Children must be put into booster seats according to their bodies. According to certain laws, you cannot smoke in the car if children are sitting in it.

4. RV Parks and Campgrounds

Canada has many different types of parks as well as camping grounds available. Many first-class resorts are available for camping as well. You can also find rustic and natural sites for camping. Every region in Canada is distinctive and has different parks. Each park will offer you beautiful scenery and atmosphere. To find out more about camping grounds, consult the Internet or contact the local tourism office. You can then formulate a plan that will help you cover a lot of spots in one trip.

5. Language

English is the most spoken language in Canada; however, French is widely spoken and understood. Certain areas such as Quebec are predominantly francophone; however, people often understand English just fine. Canada is a multicultural society, and you will find people from different parts of the world living together and speaking each other's languages. Hindi, Punjabi, Spanish, etc., are widely spoken as well.

6. Safety

Canada is one of the safest regions globally; however, it is still recommended to stay aware and be smart about safety. It is always better to be safe than sorry. Don't leave your valuables easily accessible in your vehicle, and always lock all the doors carefully. Remember, keep an eye on everything and never let your common sense falter. If you follow simple rules and regulations, you will be able to enjoy and finish your trip without any issue.

7. Internet and Cell Phone Coverage

Almost all campgrounds and RV parks in Canada offer Wi-Fi services. Certain provincial and federal campgrounds may not offer you this service as they are situated in remote areas. Internet service can also be found at cafes, libraries, and downtown centers. Cellphone coverage is great except in remote areas. In remote areas, you may have to go without cellphones. It is recommended to check the roaming rates that are applicable in Canada with your provider.

8. The Metric System

Canada follows the metric system, so everything from fuel, weight, distance, etc., will be measured using metric units such as liters, kilos, meters, etc.

9. Restaurants and Grocery Stores

Many major grocery stores are available in Canada, and almost all American foods can be found in these stores. You must try certain authentic recipes of Canada in local farmer's markets and restaurants.

10. Planning Your Route

Canada is a huge nation that stretches right from the Atlantic Ocean on the eastern end to the Pacific Ocean on the west. You can visit various forms of nature such as beautiful coastlines, tall mountains, wide-open fields, the historical and francophone culture of Quebec, etc. It is therefore recommended to select and plan a route carefully.

Chapter Eight: Driving and Operating the RV

Special Licenses

Speaking of driving, you must be nervous if this is your first time driving one. Most people will find that driving an RV can be very difficult unless you're a seasoned truck or bus driver. If you've spent your entire life up to this point driving sedans and SUVs, then this one will take a bit more time to get used to.

You should always try to start small and keep practicing until you get used to bigger and bigger rigs. Most large RV rental companies will have orientations for people renting their vehicles for the first time, but they're not going to teach you how to drive it. You're going to have to learn it by yourself.

But before we get into that, let's talk about the licenses required to drive an RV. Most of the time, the driver's license you're holding right now will suffice; however, if your rig goes over 26,000 pounds, you will need a Commercial Driving License (CDL) in some states. In other states, a non-commercial Special Driver's License is needed if your rig goes over a certain length and weight.

Weighing at 6,000 to 8,000 pounds on average, Class B's are safe. No state will stop you from driving one with your normal driver's license. The same goes with Class C's - they just weigh on average around 10,000 to 12,000 pounds. T here are Super C's, but most often than not, you won't be required to have a CDL.

For Class A's, these rigs average 13,000 to 30,000 pounds, so if you go past 26,000, you need a CDL. However, for towables, some states like California require a non-commercial class A license if you are going to tow a fifth wheel over 15,000 pounds GVWR or a trailer over 10,000 pounds GVWR.

To break it down, here are the states that require a Commercial Driver's license.

Arkansas - CDL required if your rig is over 26,000 pounds

Connecticut - Class B CDL is required if a single rig is over 26,000 pounds. Class A CDL for two or more vehicles that has a combined weight of 26,000 pounds.

Hawaii - Class B CDL is required if a single rig is over 26,000 pounds. Class A CDL for two or more vehicles that has a combined weight of 26,000 pounds.

Kansas - Class B CDL is required if a single rig is over 26,000 pounds. Class A CDL for 2 or more vehicles that has a combined weight of 26,000 pounds.

New Mexico - Class B CDL is required if a single rig is over 26,000 pounds. Class A CDL for 2 or more vehicles that has a combined weight of 26,000 pounds.

Washington, D.C. - Class B CDL is required if a single rig is over 26,000 pounds. Class A CDL for 2 or more vehicles that has a combined weight of 26,000 pounds.

Wisconsin - if your rig is over 45 feet, a CDL is required.

Driving an RV

There are three things you have to keep in mind when you're driving a bigger rig, especially when you're turning: the blind spots, the wide turns, and the rear overhang. Bigger rigs have a longer wheelbase - that's the length between the steer axle or the drive axle - so the turns need to be wider. You have to move further into the intersection before turning; sharp turns near the curb will result in your rear tires climbing over the curb. Blind spots are also bigger; you have to keep an eye on your mirrors when you're turning or switching lanes. You also have to keep in mind the RV's rear overhang when turning.

The RV's rear overhang starts at the drive axle - also known as the RV's pivot point - to the end of your RV. The sharper the wheel cut or, the sharper you turn, the larger the RV's overhang would swing out towards the opposite direction. If you turn left, the rear will swing right. This doesn't just happen to RVs - it happens on all vehicles, but it's just more pronounced in RVs because they're longer. More often than not, the miscalculation of the RV's overhang swing is the cause of accidents where drivers hit poles, signs, fire hydrants, etc.

It will definitely take some time to get used to, I know. RVs are large, cumbersome beasts for the most part. You'll find that it takes longer for them to accelerate, and they break slower too. That's why I can't stress this enough: practice makes perfect, and in driving a bigger RV, you'll have to practice a lot to get a sense of how to turn and handle your vehicle easily with hopefully no accidents. Driving a van is highly suggested - start driving with a van or a smaller Class C, especially if you have no prior experience in driving bigger vehicles - and no, your monster truck doesn't count.

That said, here are some driving tips you should know about when you start driving an RV.

Practice

Driving an RV is basically the same as when you've driven any other vehicle - same principles on how to accelerate, how to stop, how to switch gears, etc. - but the size of the RV is such a huge factor that new drivers feel like they're learning to drive all over again when they're in front of the RV's wheel for the first time.

Find yourself an empty parking lot and spend a couple of days in there practicing some rather difficult driving maneuvers. If you've found it difficult to parallel park in your SUV, then you can imagine how hard it would be to park with a big rig. Familiarize yourself with how the rig turns and feels when you're driving it because no one wants to spend their vacation stressed out while driving.

Watch your mirrors all the time. As we said before, the blind spots of your rig are larger than your normal vehicle, so when you look through your mirror, make sure that you will see most of your rig's sides easily. The last thing you want to do when you're turning or switching lanes is to crush a mini sedan.

Get a spotter when you're parking or backing up

Your rearview mirror is going to be pretty much useless, so unless you have a rearview camera mounted at the back of your rig, have someone outside to spot for you to make sure you're not hitting anything. If your rig is especially long, develop hand signals with your partner or get walkie-talkies so you won't be shouting at each other down the length of your RV.

Be aware of the weather

You should avoid driving in bad weather. An RV isn't a four-wheeldrive built for running in extreme weather conditions. Besides, the strong winds will make it difficult for you to drive. The RV is a boxy thing - it's not really aerodynamically designed. The wind resistance is only going to slow you down, so when it's raining, snowing, or hailing outside, stop and park somewhere safe first. After all, you have everything you need in your rig - you can camp literally anywhere.

You should make a habit of watching or looking for the weather forecast whenever you're out driving in your RV. It's not always going to be perfect blue skies accompanying you as you go on your epic road trips. That sunny weather can take a turn for the worse, so checking the weather app or listening to the weather reports can save you a lot of time and effort in the end as well.

It's also more expensive to repair a wrecked RV, so do your wallet a favor and stay put when the weather is bad. You'd also be saving yourself from a lot of potential Walmart overnight stays.

Know your rig's size

Be hyper-aware of the size of your rig - not just the length but also the width and the height. The roads of America are peppered with some low vertical clearance bridges. They just aren't prepared to take on bigger rigs sometimes, so be sure to know where they are and plan your route properly. Most RVs have an average height of

11 to 13 feet, so watch out for those vertical clearance signs - they're there for a reason. It's hard to make a 10-point turn on a narrow road because you can't pass the vertical clearance of a bridge.

Just as important is the rig's width. During road closures, the lanes are narrowed down significantly. Some states limit RVs with widths 8 feet and a half to the interstates, so the bottom line is, if it looks like the RV won't fit, don't push it. You'd only hit something, or worse, you'd get stuck.

So the best thing to do is to plan your route. If your RV is especially big, all the more should you stick to your planned route. This way, you won't be surprised by a low clearance bridge or tunnel appearing in front of you. There are tons of apps out there for RV route planning. Some of the good ones may charge a fee, but if you're going to live in an RV, we feel like this is one expense you won't regret paying for.

Drive slowly

Don't mind the others on the road - they're rushing, and they have smaller cars. Let them honk all they want. Slow and steady wins the race. RV driving experts recommend that when driving an RV, you shouldn't exceed 65 MPH. Not only are you staying safe, but you're also saving gas.

Keep a safe distance between you and the vehicle in front of you

An RV is heavy - it's literally a home on wheels. The brakes will not be as fast as they would be on a regular vehicle. It will take time for your RV to roll to a complete stop. You can't and don't want to do sudden stops, else everything inside your drawers will come flying out, or you'll crash into the vehicle in front of you.

Also, you should be wary about riding the brakes of the RV. Riding the brakes may cause it to overheat and malfunction - you don't need me to point out how dangerous that would be if you're going up winding roads or going cross country. Please do your brakes a huge favor - downshift first before breaking.

This is why the safest distance between you and your neighboring driver is around 400 to 500 feet - the more, the better in your case. You would need lots of space to break safely. If someone behind you is rushing and invading your personal space, lengthen the distance between you and the vehicle in front even more. That way, when the one at the back crashes into you, you can avoid crushing the vehicle upfront.

Keep right

Stay on the rightmost lane when driving, especially when you're on the highway. The RV you are driving is big and slow, so stay on the rightmost lane and let the other smaller cars fly past you. Staying on this lane will lessen your anxiety if you're stressed that you're slowing the other cars down - at least I know I do.

Not only will staying in the right lane be the safest for you and the other cars in the road, but you'll also be nearer to the shoulder so you can easily stop if there's some problem with your rig. And as a bonus, you only have to look at one side mirror: your driver's side mirror.

Now, how about the exits on the highway? If an exit is approaching, switch one lane over and let all the other vehicles go through the exit ramp. After, you can easily switch back to the right lane.

Truck stops are your friend

Normal gas stations are the bane of any new RV drivers: low-hanging roofs and tight turns. It is a sure recipe for disaster, so when you're new to driving an RV, stick to the truck stops. As the gas pumps in truck stops are built with bigger vehicles in mind, you'd have no problem maneuvering your RV in there. Get someone to spot for you when you're pulling up while you're at it, just to make sure you're not going to hit anything dangerous.

Check your engine

Always check and maintain your engine. We've already given you a list of what to pack in case of road emergencies. The most important should be the ones concerning your vehicle safety, so make room for those items. It's also advised to make a checklist and make it a point to inspect your RV before sitting behind the wheel.

Check all your lights to see if they're working and signaling properly. This includes the RV's headlights, signal lights, and tail lights.

Check your tires. You should have a portable air compressor with you in your trunk. Check your tire's pressure and tread depth.

Check your belts and hoses. There shouldn't be any cracks.

If you are towing something along, check the towing equipment and the hitch, and the safety cables.

Check for signs of any kind of leaks under your rig

Check your oils' levels, brake fluid, transmission, and coolant, and top them if needed.

Check your brakes. This includes the air brake, parking brake, and - if you're dragging a towable - also check your tow brakes.

Check other systems

And lastly, before you drive off into the sunset after checking your engines, you should also check all the other parts of your RV before you make your way out of the parking lot or campsite. An RV has a lot of miscellaneous things attached to it, like steps, awnings, etc. So you should:

Make sure your smoke and gas detectors are all in working order.

Check to see if your propane tank has any leaks.

Retract everything you pulled out when you camped and lock them so they're ready for travel. This includes awnings, steps, jacks, slide-outs, wheel blocks, etc.

Don't forget everything you placed outside when you camped. This may include your tables, chairs, pets, and other camping gear you placed outside.

If you're in a campsite with partial or full hookups, disconnect from all hookups: electrical, water, sewer, cable tv, etc.

Make sure your stove, heaters, and burners are off or anything that's powered by your propane tank.

All windows and doors should be latched. You don't want them torn off when you're on the interstate.

Check if your ladder is stowed properly.

Check your roof. Close all your vents; stow your antenna and satellites.

Close all your drawers, cabinets, and doors securely.

Switch off any electrical appliance that's connected to your 12V battery. You don't want to run out of electricity in the middle of your trip.

Check your water tanks. Fill up your freshwater tank if needed; empty your grey and black water tank as needed.

Chapter Nine: Tips & Tricks For RV Camping

Trailer Steering Trick

Here is the trick we learned if you are struggling to get the back of the trailer to go right or left on demand.

Put your hand on the bottom of the steering wheel (6 o'clock position). If you want the *back end* of the trailer to go right, move your hand (at the bottom of the steering wheel) to the right (towards the 3 o'clock position). And move your hand on the wheel towards the left (towards the 9 o'clock position) if you want the *back end* to go left.

Generally, the worst thing you can do when backing up is to turn it too hard initially and jack-knife it. Whenever we have to start over backing it up, the driver had turned too hard initially. We normally start with a small turn as soon as the trailer back end gets close to the driveway and make small adjustments after that. And keep an eye on the front of your truck to make sure you have enough clearance on that end as well as you move.

I would also recommend that you practice a few times in advance in an open area, like a large parking lot or driveaway, before adding the challenge of working around trees and tight roads.

Campsite Arrival Checklist

Remember that there is no rush. You can back up more than once to get it right. Once you are on the site:

1. Is the distance to the power and water hookups close enough to your outlets?

2. Did you give the slides enough space to expand?

3. Do you need to put one side on the risers to make it level? If the site is not level side to side about the wheels, it is a good idea to have leveling blocks, which you can buy at any RV dealer, or if you are cheap, we use a couple of 2x8 pieces that we cut to around 9 inches. You want it as long as possible, but that can still fit between the two wheels in the trailer. You put down the wood on the lower side and drive it forward a few inches until the tires rest on the blocks. This is really important if the site is heavily sloped, or everything will roll to one side, and sleeping becomes uncomfortable.

4. Park. Put the chocks for all the tires. (This is not optional. You need to have blocks in place to make sure it does not go anywhere. If you are cheap like us, we made ours out of a mini-tower of 2 x 4s. I have worked great for over a decade.)

5. Disconnect the truck from the trailer, including the hitch, safety wire, chains, and bar stabilizers. Bring extra wood to put under the tongue jack so that it does not dig into the dirt and so that it can be raised up higher if needed. We bring 4-5 blocks that are 4x4 posts cut into about 9 inches in length to be stacked if needed. (and we have almost always needed to stack them to get it level) Also, remember to release the ball from the hitch before trying to raise it up.

6. Change the tongue jack's height so that it is level from the front to the back.

7. Lower your stabilizers.

8. If you have hook-ups, connect up to the water, sewer, and power outlets.

9. Put out the slides.

10. Take out everything else you need to set up camp – chairs, tables, BBQ, etc.

Unhitching The Trailer & What To Do If You Can Not Get The Hitch And Ball Unstuck

You parked the trailer at the campsite. Good job!

The next big hurdle is unhitching the trailer from the truck.

While I mention it briefly on the previous page, you may want to add a few more details to look and feel confident on your gravel pad. Here are the steps we follow to unhitch the trailer:

1 – Block the wheels of the trailer.

2 – Disconnect the electrical plug, the breakaway switch (the very important and thin little cable), and the safety chains.

3 – Use the tongue jack to raise the hitch up a few inches. This is to take the weight off the equalizer bars.

4 – Remove the equalizer bars using the tool included with your trailer. Be careful when you snap the bars down. If there is a lot of tension, they will snap down hard, and the handle could go flying or come down hard on your thumb if you are not ready for it. Thus, the importance of step 3.

5- Crank the tongue jack back down, so that the tongue jack is sitting off the ground and all the weight is back to sitting on the hitch.

6- Now release the hitch.

There are times that the hitch does not want to release from the trailer. During our last trip, we met a family who had this problem.

They raised the hitch many inches above the neutral position, and I guess trying to have the hitch fall off with gravity. It was to the point that the trailer was sloped severely towards the back, and the hitch was high in the air.

This was a big mistake. Leaving it like that could have affected the fridge (it needs to be level when you are using it) and made it impossible to use the truck for their entire trip. Also, sleeping at that angle would have been a challenge. Overall, No Bueno.

If you cannot get it released and STUCK on the ball: (technically called the coupler, if you want to have all the technical terms while you are frustrated.)

After completing Steps 1-6, put the truck in drive and move forward about a quarter of an inch (or about as far as it will go).

If you have been driving for any time, there is a lot of pressure on the ball. We want to interfere with this pressure.

The wheel blocks have locked the trailer to move forward with the truck when you drive that tiny amount. Moving the truck VERY SLIGHTLY takes the pressure off the "coupler lock," and then it should be possible to unhitch the thing.

7 – Once the coupler is released, jack the tongue back up until the hitch is higher than the tow vehicle ball. It must be completely above the ball. Then drive the tow vehicle forward.

8 - Level the trailer as needed depending on the angle of your site.

Chapter Ten: Outdoor Kitchen Organization Tips, Tricks, And Essential Items

Whenever we see a tour of someone's RV in a video, they always show all their cutlery and plates, cups, etc., neatly tucked in a cupboard and drawer. It always amazes me that this is how they organize their camping kitchen.

The kitchen in any reasonably sized RV is super small. The counter space in my 30-foot trailer is about 8 inches, which is barely enough room to make tea, let alone an entire meal.

I realize that if you have a 45-foot fifth wheel with eight slides, you will have an island and 35 feet of counter space, where you make daily buffets for your party of 15. But for the common folk, that is not the case.

As a rule, we do NOT make meals in the trailer. We make all meals outside. What if it is raining, you ask? Then we either make the meal under a canopy or tarps, or we just say, screw it and eat out that meal.

There are many advantages to making all meals outside.

First, this leads to less mess in the trailer. We're looking at spills, crumbs and trying to navigate on multiple surface areas inside the RV. Instead, I clean up by washing the tables, rinsing them off, and turning them on their side for 5 seconds to drain them off.

Second, it gives you more space to work. I have 8 feet of outside counter space using both tables. That beats 8 inches of counter space any day of the week. I am not a super chef who can make 4 different dishes in the space of a breadbox. I need room to move, chop, mix. My trailer kitchen stores food but is not the ideal place for my prep work.

Third, since we also eat outside, it is closer to our "dining area." Eating in a trailer at the dinette is not preferable. Unless you are camping in a bubble, you will be sweeping out the dirt daily, if not more often, and using a flat mop at least once a day as well. The less frequently you need to clean the floor, the better. This is, after all, supposed to be an enjoyable trip, where you do more than just clean 200 square feet 9 times a day.

If we are not prepping inside, it means that we need to have an outdoor kitchen. This is how we set up ours to be as functional as possible.

a) Collapsible tables for food prep. I personally use two tables. Each table is four feet long. The legs fold down, and they cost about $50 each. They are stored stacked in the trailer on travel days. I make them into an "L" formation and use one for meal prep and one for temporary food storage.

If you are staying at a campsite or RV park with tighter spacing, you could put the tables up against the trailer, and if it is a really tight site, use one table instead of 2.

b) Clear plastic containers with lids for plates and cups. While your trailer looks sparkling clean in the showroom, remember that you are moving your trailer to a location full of dirt, bugs, and more dirt. I got my containers from the Dollar Store. They are about 10 inches by 18 inches. One holds cups, and one holds plates. I chose see-thru plastic to make it easy to see, which put a label on the top and side of the box to make it super clear. I use another smaller plastic container for larger utensils, such as a ladle, spatula, peeler, large knife, cheese grater, and such.

c) Cutlery Plastic Cases. I have used children's pencil cases (the rectangular ones with a flip-over lid) or smaller plastic containers with a lid (both from the Dollar Store, yes there is a cheap solution theme here) cutlery. Again, we use two containers. I sort them with one for knives and one for fork and spoons. I am not in the mood to stop and clean cutlery halfway through the process, so I bring a dozen or more of each cutlery type, which takes up space, and it can cram one container too full. Also, it's easier to find an item that way.

The need for reasonable-sized plastic containers cannot be understated if you plan to do your cooking outdoors. When we arrive, we take all the boxes out at the same time and put them on a table. We often leave them on the picnic table between uses since everything is clean and protected from the elements, thanks to the lids

One caveat is if you are camping in a place where you don't trust the neighbors not to help themselves to your stuff while you are away. Then obviously, bring in the collection when not in use. It still only takes seconds to move the stack in and out of the trailer when needed if you feel more comfortable bringing it in between meals.

d) Bar-B-Q. If you have a newer trailer with the built-in BBQ, you are already set. If not, you need to get a tabletop or collapsible BBQ. We have a small folding table to hold our BBQ. You can also use your picnic table, but then you lose space for eating.

The BBQ is used for almost all meals. It is basically a substitute oven. If you don't have an electrical hook-up, we use it to make up to 8 slices of toast at a time. The BBQ is used in almost all meals. This item is considered essential.

e) Propane Stove. Most trailers have a hook-up for an outdoor propane stove. If you don't, you will need to get a stovetop one. Often you even find a second-hand one online.

The inside trailer stove is to be used for emergencies, such as it is freezing outside one morning and you want to boil water for coffee. Then you use the indoor stove to allow you to make the coffee without venturing into the arctic air and warmup the trailer so that you will get the courage to strip down and change into your clothes for the morning.

f) 1 to 20 PoundConverterPropane Adapter Hose. This item is directly related to items (d) and (e). If you have a tabletop stove or BBQ, you will need propane, of course. Those little bottles of propane can easily deplete a bank account as they are $6 or more for each 1-pound container of propane.

But there is hope on the horizon. You can get an adapter at Wal-Mart or a hardware store that converts the stove/BBQ connection from requiring to use only the tiny canisters to now be able to use the 20-pound tanks. It costs about $30, but it will pay for itself very quickly. This changes the price from six dollars or more per pound to about a dollar a pound, which is over an 80% discount on your propane costs.

Then you can just bring the 20-pound tank with you (or take the extra tank off your trailer if the trailer holds two and you are completely out), and hook it up, and voila! Propane at a fraction of the cost. We have found that a 20-pound tank can last us up to 5 weeks of daily use, even when we use it for multiple meals each day.

g) French Press Coffeemaker. If you don't have an electrical hook-up, a coffeemaker is not an option, and either way, it can be bulky.

We use a French press to make coffee. It takes up much less space, makes coffee under a minute after the water boils, and works under all conditions. It costs about $15 and available in most kitchenware aisles. I have even found them at the Dollar Store for only a couple of bucks.

h) Dishwashing basins. After you make the mess, you have the joy of cleaning it up. Here if you have full hookups, including sewer, you have the choice of bringing all the dirty dishes inside, washing, rinsing, and drying them, and then putting them back in their bins.

However, if you don't have unlimited sewer capacity or don't want the hassle of bringing dirty dishes inside the trailer, here is what we do.

We have two plastic tubs from the Dollar Store. They are made with thicker plastic, and sometimes they even say wash bins on their labels. You want ones that can handle heavyweight, as water is not light.

One of the bins is for washing the dishes, and the other is for rinsing. I prefer round ones to squares because they fit easier in my sink when filling.

The washing bins have multiple purposes. We use them during meal prep to bring out (and bring back in) the assortment of food and spices you need to take out of the cupboards and fridge. This works better than trying to fit it all in your arms and dropping the pickles all over your last pair of clean socks.

Even if we have full hookups, we still wash, rinse and dry the dishes outside. We want the extra space outside to give enough room to the helpers. Plus, since all the dishes are stored in bins outside, it is easier to put them away.

One more thing...washing dishes with a lot of "stuff" on them is not fun on the best of days. It makes the dishwater turn very unpleasant in a hurry.

To address this, we wipe down the plates and bowls when there is a lot of mess (think spaghetti sauce, mustard, ketchup, salad dressing, BBQ sauce, etc.) with paper towels before putting the extra messy plates or bowls in the dishwater. We will either throw the dirty tissues in the garbage or use them to start the fire later that day.

Bring an extra Kleenex and or/paper towel roll to handle the increased demand. It may not be the most fun thing to do upfront, but it makes it easier to wash everything without having to change the wash water several times.

i) Coolers – Extend Your Fridge Space. I bring an extra cooler for all beverages. We fill the cooler with a bag of ice each day, and it keeps everything cold and easily available without using valuable and very limited fridge space. This gives us several more cubic feet of useable space.

j) Sorting Food by Meals. It is easier to sort the foods in your trailer according to the most-used-for-meal type. For us, breakfast has more food variety than you would think. For example, in one plastic milk crate, we store bread, peanut butter, honey, oats, sugar, coffee. It makes it easy just to need to grab the cream in the morning, throw it in the box with the rest of the breakfast items and take it outside. It is also easier when you are bringing it all back inside at the end of the meal.

k) If there is no room for an outdoor kitchen of any kind. You have to do the entire meal prep inside. If you have an electrical hook-up, I will use a crock-pot whenever possible. It allows you to do the majority of the meal prep in advance. It would also minimize the number of extra pots you have to clean. And you can heat up the leftovers the next night.

The Secret RV Fridge

Temperature Control Location

I have yet to meet anyone who knows this trick, but it works.

RV fridges generally do not have a temperature control knob, at least not one that is well-known.

However, there is a way to control your fridge's temperature if you have a fridge with steel fins as your cooling device. (The fridges with the thin columns of steel above the top row of the fridge to cool the unit.) These are the most popular type of RV fridges.

Look at the steel fin on the far-right side. There, you will find a clear or white plastic bar attached to the plate. That is, amazingly enough, the way to control the fridge temperature. The further up you move the plastic bar on the plate, the colder the fridge will get. So, if the fridge is too warm, move it up. If the milk starts freezing, move it down a bit. It also controls the freezer temperature.

Before we learned this trick, we had the bar at the bottom of the steel column, not knowing better. Like almost everyone else, we didn't even realize it was there and certainly had no idea of its true purpose. We also had all sorts of food issues not keeping as long as we would like and ice cream being too soft.

After learning of this trick, we moved that little plastic bar up the plate. The food lasted much longer, and we had, for the first time ever, hard ice cream.

Conclusion

Thanks for reaching the end of the book

There will be times when people will judge you for choosing to live in a different way from what society dictates, especially if you live in a smaller rig and plan to visit lots of cities. You'll sometimes have to fill up your jugs or tanks from drinking fountains. You'll have to learn not to mind what others think of you. You don't have to be embarrassed. There might be a lot of reasons why a person might choose to live this life other than the grand adventures offered, but as long as you're not doing anything wrong, you're good.

Some campsites have a 10-year rule, which means RVs older than ten years might not be admitted. This more or less happens on the more high-end parks, with reasons like keeping the vehicle breakdowns to a minimum, preventing electrical surges, or even keeping the park's aesthetics looking pristine. So if you're planning to rent or get an older RV, add this to the questions you need to ask the campsite first before putting down that deposit.

If you have an RV that relies a lot on solar power for electricity, the weather will rule your life. If it's cloudy for a couple of days, better drive to sunny spots or settles without electricity for a couple of days.

Find an RV where you can stand up comfortably inside. If you are on the short side, then this should be no problem for you. A lot of people underestimate how important it is to be able to stand up and walk around in a rig without bending any part of your body or hitting your head whenever you go to the bathroom, especially if you're planning to take long trips. No one wants to develop chronic back pains after a grand vacation.

If you do have back pains and are planning to go on a really long trip, seriously consider getting a good mattress for your rig, whether you're renting it or not. Your back will sing praises to thank you soon after.

Not all trucks can pull your 5th wheel, even if the dealer says so—research intensively before putting money down.

Laundromats can make clothes wear out quicker, so this is a warning to all fashionistas. Keep the expensive and delicate garments at home unless you're willing to hand wash them.

Don't go cheap on RV tires.

Don't drive when you're tired or sleepy. Take breaks now and then. The bigger the vehicle, the bigger the accident it can cause.

Bring a small fire extinguisher with you.

Everyone in the RV is required to wear a seatbelt when the vehicle is moving. Having a kitchen at the back of your vehicle is no excuse to whip up a sandwich when your RV goes 60mph in the interstate. Be safe and stay strapped in your seat. Save the snack making until you're parked.

John Bell

CAMPING COOKBOOK

A Complete Guide with Easy and Delicious Recipes to be Enjoyed in Your Camping Trip

Introduction

Camping is a great family vacation activity, teaches families about the outdoors and their environment. Camping is a way to enjoy a fun-filled, outdoor adventure safely.The purpose of camping is for fun and relaxation. But to enjoy your trip, it's important to have a basic understanding of safety. Safety is paramount when traveling with children

Camping cooking is a great way to cook outdoors over an open fire. There is no need to worry about charcoal or electrical heaters for cooking your favorite dishes in the woods

Camping is a bit more critical than home cooking because you can't order pizza if anything goes wrong. When you start cooking at the campsite, a little food preparation effort will go a long way. Not only would the meals taste healthier, but they will also be easier to prepare. Before your campsite trip, plan your dinner and snack, and make sure you don't burn your meal or get stuck with chips the first night. The plan will look very different depending on how you camp.

There is no better way than picking up a few things and going out to your ideal camping place to explore the outdoors with family and friends or even alone. It is necessary, though, to ensure that the food and water you intend to use is healthy, whether taken from home or scavenged in the wilderness. The easiest way of making a camping trip goes wrong is to ignore food hygiene. Any vacation can be spoiled by food or water poisoning, which can also contribute to harmful and long-lasting medical problems that you can almost definitely regret.

It's generally better to make some food preparation you'll be doing as safe as possible while camping. To ensure the protection of yourself and the people involved in your party, stop utilizing perishable food products and always use the necessary hygiene procedures. However, the barbecue and cookouts are a favorite of the camping culture. For this purpose, while cooking in the natural surroundings, it is necessary to watch all the appropriate safety precautions for preparing food.

The Need To Practice Proper Food Safety

If adequate safety measures are not taken, many harmful and disease-causing organisms can contaminate the food and drink. Microbiologists have reported more than 200 foodborne illnesses. Many of these infections are contagious and are caused by a combination of viruses, parasites, and bacteria. Hazardous substances and contaminants are also a big source of anxiety and may cause intense disease. The biggest threat for someone who braves the woods is a foodborne disease. For that purpose, the number one safety concern should be food hygiene and food safety.

More caution might be needed, depending on the place, time of year, and other variables. Also, contact municipal officials for any hazards of contamination that might be found in local water sources, as well as for any viruses that are likely to be borne by local wildlife. While enjoying wild game not cooked by a specialist, special caution should be taken. Until prior inspection by a certified food service official, hunters and others in a hunter's group are warned not to consume the wild game.

Keep Cold Food Cold And Hot Food Hot.

It is not necessary to overestimate the value of refrigeration. Over the decades, refrigeration has saved countless lives and is your first protection against food spoiling and inducing disease from microbes, insects, and other creatures. In the first lines of protection against foodborne disease is the propensity to chilled meats and other ingredients. Cold foods often need extra care and must at all times be held at or below 41 degrees Fahrenheit. Food can never be left out for longer than 2 hours, less than an hour if the weather is over 90 degrees F, at room / outdoor temperatures.

It is not very popular to take hot food camping because most hot food consumed outdoors is prepared on a camp stove or open fire, but it does not imply that you are not at risk. In the two-hour cycle following cooking, food cooked in the camp

must be eaten or stored in a colder location.

Choose Foods With Little To No Planning Required.

It sounds gourmet to have a steak or stuffed chicken breast but may create more issues than its value. Canned or pre-packaged foods can make life around the camp simpler and safer. Try canned chicken instead of taking in fresh chicken. For dried noodles and dehydrated vegetables that need just hot water, bring the favorite soup mixes. Several raw food alternatives require immediate planning, and that will decrease the risks of unsafe handling.

Camping Essentials

There is definitely one of the most prominent places on the campsite to enjoy healthy food outdoors. The preparation, ingenuity, and equipment required for creating gourmet meals in the open are not that challenging. Few people say that camping is uncomfortable, frustrating, and may make the food situation particularly stressful. In general, when you camp as quickly as possible, it is simpler to prepare food. Dismay using perishable foodstuffs and always follow the appropriate hygiene measures to safeguard yourself and your mates.

Kitchen Essentials Checklist at Camping

The planning, imagination, and the right equipment for gourmet meals during cooking outdoors are not that difficult. Nice food outside the campsite is one of the greatest. You will enter your campsite with an appendix about what you expect to consume in a forward-looking culture when you were at the campsite.

You just need to feed and rest afterward.

Camping Stove

A camping stove is an important piece of equipment if you are contemplating cooking on your next camping trip. A camping stove for certain cooking types will be required, whether it is a singular or dual burner, cantilevered, or table-top.

Safety is still a concern while cooking, so it's important to take all the appropriate precautions. If you are camping in tents, caravan, or motorhome, it's important not to cook in the unit because of the possible fire danger. Also, poor ventilation can contribute to a build-up of toxic carbon monoxide.

Camping Stove Gas

If you do not have any fuel to start it up, there is no point in keeping a camping stove. Different stoves need various fuel types, but it's safe and convenient to use butane (generally in a blue high-pressure cylinder) or propane (in a red cylinder).

As it is safe and quickly portable, gas is a great complement for cooking fuel. Have a glance at our guide to gas and liquid fuels before using camping petrol.

Dinnerware

It might sound like a given, but it's simple to overlook that you may need to eat and drink something. Since it is safer for the atmosphere than to use single-use paper plates and disposable cutlery, it is worth investing in any reusable dinnerware. Here is what you would need:

- Plates
- Bowls
- Cups
- Mugs
- Forks and knives
- Teaspoons and spoons
- Dishes for Serving

Pots and Pans for camping

You will need certain utensils to cook your meals, whether it's unique camping kitchen appliances or homemade cookware. On the market, there is a broad range of pots and pans available. Custom camping cookware is generally lighter, more durable, and easier to carry. If you plan to cook large quantities for many people, it is necessary to note to carry larger utensils.

Camping Kettle

Packing a kettle can help you have a cup of tea or coffee or cook some pasta or rice. There are many camping kettles on the deal, such as aluminum and stainless steel and rapidly-packable folding kettles. If you're new to camping and have decided to book onto a pitch with electricity, any kettle rated at about 2kw or less will do the job.

Cooking Utensils

No matter which recipe you are trying, you will, at some stage, require knives for slicing, wooden spoons for mixing, and spatulas for tossing. Here is a rundown of what you would need:

- Wooden spoon
- Large spoons
- Tongs
- Spatula
- Whisk
- Sharp knife
- Chopping board

Water Container

It is a concern of comfort to have a complete bottle of water. To refill the container and then use the provision each time you need it, use a tap at your camping site. You can purchase foldable water containers and those with taps from most outdoor stores, which are simple to pack, move, and use.

First Aid Kit

Whenever it comes to camping, protection always comes first. A small first aid kit

is important for every camping trip. When cooking food, burns and cuts are fairly normal, and plasters and bandages may be very helpful.

Here's a list of what you need in the kit:

- A variety of plasters
- Disposable sterile gloves
- A variety of bandages
- Tweezers
- Scissors
- Wipes for cleaning
- Thermometer
- Sticky tape
- Antiseptic cream
- Pain relievers

Folding Toaster For Camping

Affordable, filling, and convenient, toast is an excellent camping meal to eat. There's no reason to carry the toaster with you from home if you have a foldable camping toaster. It's easy, healthy, and great to cook with a camping toaster toasting bread, breakfast sandwiches, and teacakes and melting the cheese in your toast.

Table Camping

You bought all the ingredients, brought all the camping equipment for cooking with you, accompanied a recipe, served it on plates, but where are you planning to eat it? Gather your family or mates around the camping table and make mealtime a shared experience. Camping tables can adapt too; just use the table to arrange a board game or glean everybody round for a game of cards.

Bin Bags

A clean camp is a pleasant camp. Put all the garbage in huge bags and leave

your campsite's area clean and clear; this would decrease the likelihood of predators having an interest and improve the confidence of all in the camp. The camping code of "leave no trace" is crucial to keep in mind, so you can do your hardest to end up leaving your pitch in the same condition as you find it in.

Washing Up Equipment

A healthy routine to fall into is to keep the pitch tidy. Don't encourage washing up to sit around, use the abundant washing facilities, and have a talk with your fellow campers whilst you're at it. It's also a perfect meeting spot. If you don't have the essentials for cleaning up the equipment, the cookware can get dirty. Here is what you would need:

- Washing up liquid
- Towels
- Scouring pad
- Sponge
- Dish-cloth

Storage of Food

You would maintain your food balanced and your atmosphere orderly by using a range of containers. By putting them chilled in Tupperware in your cool box, putting your surplus food in containers, and reusing it the next day, keep your ingredients new. Sheets of beeswax will even help keep food fresh if you don't have any containers.

The Chimney Starter

This foldable compact chimney can make the coal burn in moments without the need for harmful burning lighter fluid, extremely great while using charcoals.

Portable grill

While most campsites have campfires with grates, their state may be less than enticing. It is possible to position this portable grill on top of the campground grill (with collapsing legs) or use it independently (when freestanding). If free camping on public grounds, where there are no grill grates that cover fire pits, may be beneficial.

Thermometer with Quick-Reading

Knowing the precise condition of a slice of meat or the Dutch oven's interior condition may be useful when you're just starting to cook outside. It's easier to know unless you evolve the senses to go through intuition. A perfect method to guess as the steak is done cooking or not is this probe thermometer.

You can actually get away without one if you are new to camping, but it's certainly the key to make things very pleasant.

Cast Iron Skillet With A Lid

This is the camp kitchen MVP. On a camp burner, over a campfire, or snuggled in a bed of charcoal, cast iron may be used. It has an inherently non-stick structure, superior heat preservation, and is essentially indestructible.

Non-Stick Skillet

It is debatable whether or not this is a "necessary" component of camp cooking equipment. Without it, you should get by. But whether you prepare scrambled eggs, pancakes, tuna, or something else that's sensitive, there's no substitution for a decent skillet that doesn't stick. This skillet would last for years if paired with a fitting silicone or wooden spatula.

Dutch Oven

One of the most valuable items of camp cookware that you will own is a Dutch oven. If you can picture it, you can make it in a Dutch oven. Sauté, steam, boil, roast, and bake. A flat rim lid helps you mount charcoals on top, while underneath, you can nestle coals with support legs on the bottom.

Egg Holder

There are many dubious, almost gimmicky camping products out there, but it's worth a plastic egg holder. Before we planned to have one of these, we missed a lot of good eggs.

Streamline

After cleaning your dishes, disinfect against bacteria and viruses, add one of

these tablets to your rinse bucket. It's more potent than old-fashioned chlorine, and on the skin, it's much gentler.

Breakfast

Campfire Breakfast

Preparation time: 20 minutes

Cooking time: 10 minutes

Servings: 5

Ingredients:

- Four large eggs and ½ cup milk
- 1 pound refrigerated hash browns, thawed
- 1 cup chopped ham
- 2 cups shredded cheddar
- ½ tablespoon butter, for greasing the foil

Directions

1. Crack the eggs into a resealable plastic bag and add the milk.
2. Season with salt and pepper.
3. Add the hash browns, ham, and cheese to the bag. Carefully manipulate the bag to combine the ingredients.
4. Butter four squares of aluminum foil.
5. Divide the mixture from the plastic bag between the pieces of foil.
6. Fold it snugly, and seal.

7. Place the packets on a grill or near a campfire, and cook for about 10 minutes.

8. Serve when the eggs are set, and the cheese is melted.

Nutrition*:*

Calories 442, total fat 22 g, carb 35 g, Protein 24 g, sodium 1015 mg

Yummy Cobbler

Preparation time: 20 minutes

Cooking time: 10 minutes

Servings: 5

Ingredients:

- 2 ⅓ cups biscuit mix
- ½ cup sweetened almond milk, vanilla flavor
- ½ tablespoon butter, for coating
- 6 fresh peaches, chopped
- 1 cup strawberries, hulled and chopped

Directions

1. Before leaving for camping, combine the biscuit mix and milk in a large, sturdy, resealable bag. Seal the bag.
2. When you are ready to cook, knead the bag with your hands until the ingredients are combined.
3. Butter a large cast-iron skillet.
4. Pour in the fruits, and top them with the batter.
5. Cover the pan snugly with foil, and let it cook over the campfire for about 45 minutes.
6. Once the biscuit topping is no longer doughy, the cobbler is ready.
7. Cool for a few minutes before serving.

Nutrition:

Calories 118, total fat 12.2 g, carb 17 g, Protein 8.1 g, sodium 896 mg

Pancakes

Preparation time: 5 minutes

Cooking time: 20 minutes

Servings: 6

Ingredients:

- 2 cups pancake mix, plain
- Water, for mixing
- 1 cup blueberries for topping
- 1 cup bananas for topping
- 1 cup strawberries for topping
- 1 cup whipping cream for topping.

Directions:

1. At home, combine the pancake mix with enough water to make the desired consistency.
2. Pour the batter into a clean condiment bottle, and seal.
3. At the campsite, heat a skillet over the fire or grill.
4. Squeeze some batter onto the pan, cook until bubbles appear, and then flip.
5. When the other side is cooked, serve with the fruit and cream toppings.

Nutrition

Calories 317, total fat 10 g, Carb 63 g, Protein 8.4 g, sodium 898 mg

Dutch Oven Scrambled Eggs and Biscuits Recipe

Preparation time: 20 minutes

Cooking time: 10 minutes

Servings: 5

Ingredients:

- 1 large onion, chopped
- 1 bell pepper, chopped
- 4 eggs
- 1 package prepared biscuit dough
- ¼ cup cheddar cheese, grated

Directions

1. Before leaving for camping, in a large bowl, combine the onion, pepper, eggs; whisk well.

2. Pour the mixture into any clean condiment bottle, and seal.

3. Prepare the fire using charcoal coals or wood until the coals are hot enough to cook with.

4. Place the cast-iron Dutch oven on the hot coals, and shift the coals around the oven. Let it sit for a few minutes to heat.

5. Add the oil to the oven and let it get hot. Tip the pot, so the oil coats the bottom.

6. Pour the egg mixture from the bottle into the Dutch oven. Cover, and let it cook for a few minutes.

7. Grease the lid of the oven with a generous amount of oil and spread it evenly.

8. Open the biscuit package and brush both sides of the rolls with vegetable oil.

9. Place the oiled biscuits on top of the greased oven lid.

10. Place the aluminum foil over the top to keep the heat in...

11. Remove the lid once in a while to stir the eggs, and place it back on again.

12. Once everything is cooked, sprinkle cheese on top of the eggs and let it melt.

Nutrition: Calories 256, total fat 16.6 g, Carb 19.2 g, Protein 9.5 g, sodium 353 mg

Eggs Benedict Casserole

Preparation time: 10 minutes

Cooking time: 25 minutes

Servings: 5

Ingredients:

- 6 English muffins, cut into small pieces
- 10 ounces turkey bacon, cut into pieces
- 6 large eggs, or 1 cup egg beaters
- 2 cups milk
- Oil spray for greasing

Directions

1. Spray the Dutch oven with oil and set it in the coals to heat.
2. Combine the English muffin pieces with the bacon in the Dutch oven.
3. In a mixing bowl, combine the egg beaters, milk, mustard.
4. Pour this batter on top of the muffin and bacon mixture in the pot, and jiggle the pot, so it soaks in evenly.
5. Let it cook until the eggs are set.
6. Serve, and enjoy.

Nutrition: Calories 302, total fat 9.7 g, Carb 30 g, Protein 23 g, Sodium 866 mg

Dutch Oven Eggs Baked in Avocados

Preparation time: 15 minutes

Cooking time: 10 minutes

Servings: 4

Ingredients:

- 4 ripe avocados
- 8 eggs
- Red pepper flakes
- 6 tablespoons hot sauce
- 1 cup salsa

Directions

1. Slice the avocados and remove the seeds. Scoop out enough of the avocado flesh as needed for the egg to fit. Lay the avocados on a flat surface.
2. Crack an egg into each avocado half.
3. Place all the filled avocados into the Dutch oven.
4. Cover the Dutch oven with the lid and place it on the coals for about 15 minutes, rotating every 5 minutes.
5. Serve with hot sauce and salsa.

Nutrition

Calories 377, total fat 32 g, carb 16.4 g, Protein 10.6 g, sodium 758 mg

Preparation time: 20 minutes

Cooking time: 10 minutes

Servings: 5

Ingredients:

- 6 eggs
- 1 cup broccoli, chopped
- 1 cup mushrooms, chopped
- 1 cup tomatoes, diced
- 1 cup cheddar, shredded

Directions

1. Whisk the eggs in a large mixing bowl, and fold in all the other ingredients EXCEPT the cheese.
2. Pour this mixture into a foil-covered pie plate.
3. Place the pie plate in the Dutch oven, cover, and place the oven over the coals or campfire (on a rack).
4. Cook 25 minutes, or until the eggs are set.
5. Just before serving, sprinkle the cheese over the quiche and let it melt.

Nutrition

Calories 192, total fat 15.3 g, Carb 3.2 g, Protein 11.3 g, sodium 186 mg

Australian Damper

Preparation time: 20 minutes

Cooking time: 10 minutes

Servings: 5

Ingredients:

- 3 ½ cups self-rising flour
- 1 tablespoon lemon zest
- Salt, to taste
- ¾ cup almond milk, unsweetened
- 2 teaspoons sugar
- ¼ cup butter
- Pinch cinnamon

Directions

1. At home, combine all the listed ingredients to make a soft dough, and place it in a large plastic container.

2. To bake the bread, take out the dough from the container and knead it on a clean, floured, flat surface until smooth. Shape it into a round loaf.

3. Preheat a Dutch oven over the coals.

4. Grease a sheet of aluminum foil with oil and dust it with flour.

5. Place the loaf on the foil, and carefully place it in the Dutch oven.

6. Cover, and arrange a few coals on top. Let it cook for about 35 minutes until it sounds hollow when you tap on the bottom.

Nutrition

Calories 424, total fat 16.5 g, Carb 60 g, Protein 8.6 g, sodium 91 mg

Country Breakfast

Preparation time: 20 minutes

Cooking time: 45 minutes

Servings: 5

Ingredients:

- 1 pound pork sausage
- 2 cups frozen hash browns
- 12 eggs
- 2 cups cheddar cheese, shredded
- 1 container prepared biscuit dough

Directions

1. Place the Dutch oven over hot coals and cook the sausages in it until the meat is golden brown. Drain most of the fat.

2. Spoon or shake the prepared hash browns over the sausage.

3. Crack about 12 eggs over the hash browns, and sprinkle on the cheddar cheese.

4. Arrange the biscuits over the cheese.

5. Cover the Dutch oven, and place hot coals on the lid.

6. Cook for 45 minutes or until the eggs are set.

Nutrition: Calories 446, total fat 29.1 g, Carb 19.4 g, Protein 25.7 g, sodium 36 mg

Breakfast Omelet

Preparation time: 20 minutes

Cooking time: 30 minutes

Servings: 5

Ingredients:

- 1 tablespoon butter
- 4 slices turkey bacon, chopped
- 8 eggs, beaten
- 1 cup cherry tomatoes, halved
- 1 cup baby spinach, chopped

Directions

1. Place a frying pan on a rack over hot coals, and melt the butter in it.
2. Add the turkey bacon and cook for 5 minutes, or until crisp.
3. Pour the eggs into the pan, and add the tomatoes and spinach.
4. When the eggs begin to set, gently left the omelet's edge and allowed the liquid egg to flow under the cooked layer. Repeat until the omelet is set. Do not stir.

Nutrition

Calories 316, total fat, 24 g, Carb 10 g, Protein 18.2 g, sodium 410 mg

Crab & Fennel Spaghetti

Preparation time: 10 minutes

Cooking time: 50 minutes

Servings: 4

Ingredients:

- 160 g of mixed brown and white crabmeat from sustainable sources
- 1 fresh red chili
- 1 Fennel bulb
- 150 g of dried spaghetti
- 160 g of mixed cherry tomatoes

Directions:

1. Place the Dutch oven on medium-low heat. Trim the fennel, pick any leafy tops and reserve them, then halve the bulb and slice it finely. Put a tbsp of butter in the oven and cook for 5 minutes with the lid on.

2. Meanwhile, cook the pasta in the Dutch oven of boiling salted water according to the packet instructions, then drain and reserve a mug of the cooking liquid.

3. Slice the chili thinly, stir in the dutch oven and cook uncovered until soft and moist, occasionally stirring.

4. Cut the tomatoes into the oven for 2 minutes, followed by the crab meat, and drained pasta 1 minute later.

Season with sea salt and black pepper, sprinkle with one tablespoon of extra virgin butter, and sprinkle over any reserved fennel tops, if possible, with a reserved cooking water splash. Enjoy!

Nutrition

Calories 234, total fat 14.5 g, Carb 60 g, Protein 8.6 g, sodium 91 mg

Epic Rib-Eye Steak

Preparation time: 10 minutes

Cooking time: 30 minutes

Servings: 4

Ingredients:

- 350 g mixed mushrooms
- Four sprigs of fresh rosemary
- 1 600 g jar of quality white beans
- 600 g, (ideally 5cm thick) piece of rib-eye steak, fat removed
- Four cloves of garlic

Directions

1. Place your Dutch oven on medium-high heat.

2. Rub the steak with a pinch of sea salt and black pepper all over, then sear on all sides for a minimum of 10 minutes, so you get the right color on the outside and keep it medium rare in the center, or cook to your liking, occasionally turning with tongs.

3. In the meantime, strip off the rosemary leaves' sprigs, cut and finely slice the garlic, and tear any more giant mushrooms. Transfer to a plate when the steak is finished and cover with tin foil.

4. Reduce heat to medium under the Dutch oven and crisp the rosemary for 30 seconds, then add garlic and mushrooms, then you cook for 8 minutes or always toss until golden.

5. Add 1 tbsp. of red wine vinegar and cook for 5 minutes, then season to perfection.

6. Pour over any remaining juices. Slice and serve with a little extra virgin butter at the table, if you like.

Nutrition: Calories 124, total fat 16.5 g, Carb 60 g, Protein 8.6 g, sodium 91 mg

Quinoa, Everyday Dals, And Avocado

Preparation time: 10 minutes

Cooking time: 35 minutes

Servings: 4

Ingredients:

- 1 Bag Maya Kaimal Everyday Dals of your choosing

- Half cup of quinoa (if you want more quinoa, then double the amount of rice and the amount of water)

- 1 avocado

- 1 cup of water

Directions:

1. You're going to use the same pot to heat the Dals and cook the quinoa.

2. Cook the quinoa first. Add the quinoa to the dish, cover with 1 cup of water and a little salt, then bring to a boil. Cover your pot once it has boiled and reduced it to medium-low heat and simmer until the water is absorbed into the quinoa for about 15-20 minutes. Then pass the quinoa to your bowls for cooking.

3. While your oven is still warm, add the Everyday Dals and heat them for about 5 minutes (until they are cooked through), then serve on top of your quinoa.

4. Top with some avocado and enjoy.

Nutrition

Calories 124, total fat 11.5 g, Carb 60 g, Protein 8.6 g, sodium 91 mg

Spiced Scones

PreparationTime: 15 minutes

CookingTime: 10 minutes

Servings: 6

Ingredients

- 2 cups self-rising flour
- 1 teaspoon cumin
- ⅛ teaspoon red pepper flakes, or to taste
- ¼ teaspoon salt
- 2 tablespoons butter
- ¾ cup milk

Directions

1. In a bowl, combine flour, cumin, chili, and salt.

2. Rub in butter until coarse-textured.

3. Add milk and mix.

4. Press out on a floured surface to make a ¾-inch thick round.

5. Cut into 6 wedges.

6. Cook in a nonstick frying pan or well-seasoned skillet over medium heat until browned and cooked through (about 5 minutes on each side).

Nutrition

Calories 186, Carbs 31.4 g, Fat 4.8 g, Protein 1.7 g, Sodium 670 mg

Breakfast Scramble

Preparation Time: 5 minutes

Cooking Time: 15 minutes

Servings: 2

Ingredients

- 4 small red potatoes, diced
- ¼ cup water
- 1 tablespoon olive oil
- Pinch of salt
- 4 large eggs, beaten
- 1 tablespoon milk
- 1 scallion, thinly sliced
- ⅓ cup grated cheese
- 1 tablespoon fresh thyme or herb of choice, chopped

Directions

1. Combine potatoes, water, oil, and salt in a nonstick frying pan or well-seasoned skillet.

2. Cover and cook over high heat until almost all the water has dried out and potatoes begin to sizzle in the oil (about 5 minutes).

3. Remove lid and flip potatoes, cooking until lightly browned (about 5 minutes).

4. Beat the eggs and milk in a bowl. Then pour over the potatoes.

5. Add sliced scallion and mix to scramble until set (about 3 minutes).

6. Remove from heat and sprinkle with cheese and herbs.

7. Let sit until cheese melts (about 1 minute) and serve.

Nutrition

Calories 342, Carbs 15.5 g, Fat 22.7 g, Protein 19.3 g, Sodium 425 mg

Breakfast Cinnamon Rolls

Preparation Time: 10 minutes

Cooking Time: 20–30 minutes

Servings: 6

Ingredients

- 2 (7½-ounce) packages of buttermilk biscuits
- ¼ cup butter, melted or softened to a spreadable consistency
- ¾ cup brown sugar, packed
- 1 teaspoon cinnamon
- ½ cup nuts or raisins (optional)

Frosting

- 1½ cups powdered sugar
- ¼ cup butter softened
- 1 teaspoon vanilla extract
- 2 tablespoons milk or a little more to get the right consistency

Directions

1. Heat coals until very hot for a 2- to 2¾- quart Dutch oven (about 8-inch diameter), set aside five coals for the bottom and 11 for the top.

2. Spray with nonstick spray, or rub the inside with a little oil.

3. Remove the biscuits from the packages and roll them out thinly.

4. Spread evenly with melted butter.

5. Sprinkle as evenly as possible with sugar, cinnamon, and nuts or raisins (if using).

6. Roll into rods. Note: These may be made in advance, wrapped in plastic, and frozen; allow them to thaw out during the trip.

7. Arrange in the Dutch oven, cutting as needed to make them fit.

8. Position over coals and place lid with coals on top.

9. Check about 18 minutes into cooking. Adjust the heat by removing or adding coals, as needed. Rotate the Dutch oven to ensure even heating.

10. Rolls should be done in 20–30 minutes. It should be fragrant and no longer doughy.

11. Remove from heat and let cool while you prepare the frosting (about 5 minutes).

12. Combine the sugar, butter, and vanilla. Gradually add the milk until the desired consistency is attained. It should be thick and pourable but not watery.

13. Drizzle over cooked rolls, or cut into pieces and drizzle with frosting individually.

Nutrition: Calories 656, Carbs 112.7 g, Fat 25.8g, Protein 5.7 g, Sodium 994 mg

Eggs with Beans and Tomatoes

Preparation Time: 5 minutes

Cooking Time: 12–15 minutes

Servings: 2

Ingredients

- 2 tablespoons olive or canola oil
- 1 medium red onion, minced
- 2 teaspoons cumin
- ½ teaspoon red pepper flakes, or to taste
- Salt and pepper, to taste
- 1 (14-ounce) can diced tomatoes
- ½ (15-ounce) can cannellini beans
- 4 eggs

Fresh herbs of choice (like rosemary, basil, or sage), chopped

Directions

1. Heat oil in a nonstick pan or cast-iron skillet over medium heat.

2. Add onion and spices and sauté until fragrant (about 1 minute).

3. Season with salt and pepper and add tomatoes and beans.

4. Continue cooking, with occasional stirring, until onion is tender (about 5 minutes). Make four depressions in the mixture and crack an egg into each.

5. Cover and let cook until eggs are desired doneness (about 2–5 minutes).

6. Season again, as needed, and sprinkle with herbs.

7. Serve while hot.

Nutrition

Calories 354 Carbs 21.1 g Fat 23.2 g Protein 17.9 g Sodium 1028 mg

Basic Hobo Pie

Preparation Time: 5 minutes

Cooking Time: 1–3 minutes

Servings: 5–6

Ingredients

1 loaf bread, sliced thickly into squares

¼ cup pizza sauce

Mozzarella cheese, sliced thinly or shredded

10–15 slices pepperoni, chopped

¼ cup butter, softened, or nonstick cooking spray

Directions

1. To prevent sticking, butter the bread slices that will be on the outer sides of the sandwiches, or simply spray the inside of the hobo pie maker with nonstick cooking spray.

2. Lay a slice, buttered side down (if not using nonstick spray) on the hobo pie maker.

3. Layer with pizza sauce (be sparing, as too much will spill out and burn), cheese, and pepperoni.

4. Top with the second slice of bread, buttered side up (if using butter).

5. Wrap in aluminum foil, if desired, for easier cleanup.

6. Close pie maker and place over coals, turning now and then until bread is toasted (about 1–3 minutes; heat from campfires varies a lot).

Other suggested Hobo Pie variations:

- Chocolate and marshmallows (s'mores)
- blueberry pie filling and butter or cream cheese
- ham and cheese
- peach pie filling and marshmallow
- peanut butter, marshmallow, and chocolate (rocky road)
- Nutella and strawberries
- sausage, egg, and cheese
- tuna and cheese
- use biscuit dough instead of bread

Nutrition (per serving)

Calories 220 Carbs 25.7 g Fat 8.8 g Protein 9.1 g Sodium 558 mg

Grilled Roast Beef Paninis

Preparation Time: 5 minutes

Cooking Time: 2 minutes

Servings: 1–2

Ingredients

- 2 slices of Italian bread (like ciabatta or Michetti)
- 1 tablespoon aioli garlic mustard
- 2 slices roast beef
- 2 slices provolone cheese
- ½ green pepper, grilled (optional)
- 2 tablespoons butter

Directions

1. Spread aioli over one side of each bread slice.
2. Place roast beef, cheese, and green pepper (if using) over one slice.
3. Place remaining bread slice on top.
4. Butter the outside of the bread slices.
5. Wrap in foil and place on grill or in hobo pie maker.
6. Grill until done (about 1–3 minutes, depending on heat from the campfire).

Nutrition (per serving)

Calories 349 Carbs 10.1 g Fat 24 g Protein 23.7 g Sodium 745 mg

Preparation Time: 5–10 minutes

Cooking Time: 0 minutes

Servings: 2

Ingredients

- ¾ cup quick-cooking or instant oats
- ¼ cup powdered milk
- ⅓ cup raisins or dried apple bits
- ⅓ cup unsalted mixed nuts, chopped
- 2 teaspoons unsalted shelled sunflower seeds (optional)
- 1½ tablespoons brown sugar
- ½ teaspoon cinnamon
- 2 cups boiling water

Directions

1. Prepare in advance: Combine ingredients except for the boiling water in a Ziploc bag, shaking to mix. Set aside until ready for use.

2. To serve, place the mixture in a bowl and add boiling water. Let sit for 2 minutes. Mix and serve.

Nutrition (per serving)

Calories 343 Carbs 54.2 g Fat 14.4 g Protein 8.5 g Sodium 93 mg

Dutch Oven Pizza

Preparation Time: 20 minutes

Cooking Time: 15 minutes

Servings: 12 (yield: 2 pizzas

Ingredients

- Canola oil, for greasing, or nonstick cooking spray
- 1 tube pre-made pizza crust, divided
- 1 cup tomato or pizza sauce, divided
- 3 cups mozzarella cheese, shredded, divided
- ½ cup cheddar cheese, grated, divided
- Dash of garlic powder
- Salt and pepper, to taste
- 1 medium onion, sliced, divided
- 12 ounces pepperoni slices, divided

Directions

1. Heat up coals in a fire pit, shifting them to heat evenly.

2. Grease a Dutch oven.

3. Roll out the tube of dough and divide into 2.

4. Spread one piece over the bottom of the Dutch oven, pressing and patching if needed. Note: If you want two pizzas but only have one Dutch oven, line with aluminum foil or an aluminum pie pan so that you can easily remove the first when cooked and then add the second one.

5. Spread half of the sauce over the dough.

6. Season with garlic powder, salt, and pepper.

7. Arrange half of pepperoni and half of onion on top.

8. Place over hot coals.

9. Place lid and add about 8 coals on top.

10. Cook until crust is lightly browned and no longer doughy (about 10 minutes). Meanwhile, prepare the second pizza on a sheet of foil or in an aluminum foil pie pan using the remaining ingredients (remember to leave out the cheese for now).

11. Sprinkle the first pizza with the cheese and replace the lid. Add a few more pieces of coal to melt the cheese faster.

12. Remove from coals, let cool slightly, and remove pizza from the Dutch oven.

13. Carefully place the second pizza into the Dutch oven and bake as above.

Nutrition (per serving)

Calories 329 Carbs 20.3 g Fat 21.9 g Protein 17.3 g Sodium 1106 mg

Simple Pizza Turnovers

Preparation Time: 5 minutes

Cooking Time: 15 minutes

Servings: 8

Ingredients

8–16 slices pepperoni, diced

¼ cup shredded mozzarella cheese

3–4 tablespoons pizza or tomato sauce, or as needed

1 tube flaky biscuit dough (to make 8 biscuits)

2 tablespoons butter (optional)

Directions

1. In a bowl, mix pepperoni and mozzarella.

2. Add pizza sauce gradually until pepperoni and cheese begin to stick together.

3. Flatten a biscuit and place a small amount in the middle. Do the same for the rest of the biscuits, distributing the filling as equally as possible.

4. Fold over and press edges together to seal.

5. Arrange on a nonstick pan or skillet and place over medium heat.

6. Melt butter in the pan and swirl to spread if using.

7. When the bottom is lightly browned, flip over to brown the other side (about 10–12 minutes total).

Nutrition

Calories 221 Carbs 25.1 g Fat 11 g Protein 5.6 g Sodium 774 mg

Poultry

Classic Chicken "Stir Fry"

Preparation time: 20 minutes

Cooking time: 10 minutes

Servings: 5

Ingredients:

- 4 cups cooked chicken, chopped
- 2 cups rice, cooked
- 1 green bell pepper, sliced
- 1 cup broccoli florets, chopped
- Cooking spray

Directions

1. In a large bowl, combine the chicken, rice, green pepper, broccoli. Mix well.

2. Create five double-layer rectangles of foil, and coat them with oil or cooking spray.

3. Divide the chicken mixture among the pieces of foil. Fold up the sides and create packets. Seal well.

4. Place the packets over warm coals for about 15 minutes.

Nutrition

Calories 514, total fat 5.1 g, Carb 66 g, Protein 46 g, Sodium 1207 mg

Preparation time: 30 minutes

Cooking time: 10 minutes

Servings: 5

Ingredients:

- 4 boneless, skinless chicken breast halves
- ¾ cup balsamic vinegar
- ¼ teaspoon soy sauce
- ½ cup pesto
- ½ cup honey mustard sauce

Directions

1. Place the chicken, vinegar, soy sauce, salt, and pepper in a Ziploc® bag. Let it sit for a few minutes.

2. Heat the grill over medium, and cook the chicken until it is browned on both sides and cooked through.

3. Serve with pesto and honey mustard sauce.

Nutrition

Calories 432, total fat 25 g, Carb 3.4 g, Protein 45 g, sodium 375 mg

Preparation time: 20 minutes

Cooking time: 10 minutes

Servings: 5

Ingredients:

- 1 (4-pound) fryer chicken
- ½ cup lemon juice
- 2 tablespoons vegetable oil
- 2 teaspoons thyme
- 1 teaspoon rosemary

Directions

1. Preheat the grill over a hot bed of coals.
2. Cut the chicken into four servings.
3. Remove any skin.
4. Combine the lemon juice, oil, thyme, and rosemary in a bowl, and brush it over the chicken—season with salt and pepper.
5. Grill the chicken, cavity-side down, and turn after a few minutes.
6. Baste the chicken with the sauce repeatedly while cooking.

7. Once the chicken is golden brown and cooked through, remove it from the heat.

Nutrition

Calories 123, total fat 17.2 g, Carb 10.2 g, Protein 82 g, sodium 631 mg

Chicken Kebabs

Preparation time: 50 minutes

Cooking time: 10 minutes

Servings: 5

Ingredients:

- 2 pounds boneless, skinless chicken breasts
- 6 ounces mushrooms, trimmed
- 2 unpeeled oranges, cut into 12 wedges
- ⅓ cup vegetable oil
- 1–2 teaspoons curry powder

Directions

1. Slice the chicken into long pieces. Thread the pieces on wooden skewers, alternating with mushroom and orange pieces.

2. Once finished, place the skewers in a shallow plastic dish.

3. Pour this mixture over the skewers, making sure they are well coated. Allow them to marinate for 30 minutes.

4. Grill the kebabs over medium coals, turning after 5 minutes.

5. When they are golden brown and cooked through, they are ready to serve.

Nutrition

Calories 231, total fat 13.5 g, carb 7.7g, Protein 45 g, sodium 132 mg

Chicken and Potatoes

Preparation time: 15 minutes

Cooking time: 35 minutes

Servings: 5

Ingredients:

- 5 large chicken breasts
- 5 small potatoes, cut into ½-inch slices
- 1 red onion, chopped
- 1 cup prepared barbecue sauce
- 1 teaspoon sesame seeds

Directions

1. Place the cast-iron Dutch oven on hot coals.

2. Shift the coals around the oven.

3. Add the chicken, potatoes, onions, and barbecue sauce, and stir.

4. Cover the oven with the lid and place 12 hot coals on the top. Let it cook for 35 minutes.

5. Once done, serve with a sprinkle of sesame seeds on top.

Nutrition

Calories 181 total fat 11, Carb 47 g, Protein 24.6 g, sodium 752 mg

Creamy Santa Fe Chicken

Preparation Time: 5 minutes

Cooking Time: 30 minutes

Servings: 4

Ingredients:

- 1 pound chicken tenders

- 1 tablespoon butter

- 2 cup fresh corn kernels

- 2 cups salsa verde (fresh or jarred)

- 1 cup sour cream

Directions

1. Preheat oven to 350°F/177°C.

2. Add the butter to a skillet and heat over medium.

3. Add the chicken tenders and brown for 1-2 minutes per side. Add the corn kernels and cook for an additional 2 minutes.

4. Transfer the chicken and corn to a 9"x9" baking dish.

5. Pour the salsa verde over the chicken and bake for approximately 30 minutes. Remove from the oven and stir in the sour cream.

6. Serve immediately over rice or in tortilla shells, if desired.

Nutrition: Calories 128, total fat 13.2 g, carb 77 g, Protein 8.1 g, sodium 896 mg

Preparation time: 5 minutes

Cooking time: 30 minutes

Servings: 4

Ingredients:

- 4 boneless, skinless chicken breasts
- 1 tablespoon butter
- 2 cups cherry tomatoes, quartered
- 1 cup fresh mint leaves, torn
- 1 lemon, juiced, and zested

Directions

1. Season the chicken breasts with salt and pepper.

2. Heat the butter in a sauté pan over medium-high heat. Cook until browned on each side, approximately 5-7 minutes per side, depending upon thickness.

3. Add the tomatoes, mint leaves, lemon juice, and one teaspoon of the lemon zest. Reduce heat to medium and cook, stirring gently, until tomatoes begin to soften. Some of their natural juices are released, approximately 5 minutes.

4. Remove from heat and season with additional salt and pepper, if desired.

Nutrition: Calories 128, total fat 13.2 g, carb 77 g, Protein 8.1 g, sodium 896 mg

Rosemary Chicken Bake

Preparation Time: 5 minutes

Cooking Time: 40 minutes

Servings: 4

Ingredients:

- 4 bone-in chicken breasts, skin removed
- 1 tablespoon butter
- 2 cups chicken stock
- 1 lemon, sliced
- 2 fresh rosemary sprigs

Directions

1. Preheat oven to 375°F/191°C

2. Add the butter to a skillet and heat over medium-high heat. Add the chicken to the skillet and cook until slightly browned, approximately 3-4 minutes per side.

3. Remove the chicken from the skillet and place it in a baking dish. Add ¼ cup of the chicken stock and one rosemary sprig to the chicken. Place in the oven and bake for 25-30 minutes, or until juices run clear.

4. Meanwhile, add the remaining chicken stock, rosemary, and lemon slices to the pan that the chicken was browned in. Turn heat to medium-high and bring to a gentle boil while stirring constantly. Boil for one minute before reducing heat to low. Simmer for ten minutes. Remove rosemary sprig and keep sauce warm over gentle heat.

5. Remove chicken from the oven and transfer to serving plates—spoon sauce, including lemon slices, over each chicken piece.

6. Serve immediately.

Nutrition:

Calories 428, total fat 13.2 g, carb 77 g, Protein 8.1 g, sodium 896 mg

Chicken with Cornbread Stuffing

Preparation time: 5 minutes

Cooking time: 4 hours

Servings: 4

Ingredients:

- 4 boneless skinless chicken breasts
- 3 cups dried cornbread crumbs (prepackaged or fresh)
- 2 cups chicken stock
- ½ cup celery, finely diced
- 1 teaspoon dried sage

Directions

1. Season the chicken with salt and pepper, then place in a layer among the bottom of a crock pot.
2. In a bowl combine the cornbread crumbs, celery, and sage. Add additional salt and pepper, if desired.
3. Add the cornbread mixture over the top of the chicken.
4. Pour the chicken stock over the cornbread mixture, stirring if necessary to make sure corn bread is saturated.
5. Cover crock pot and heat on high for 4-6 hours, or until chicken juices run clear.

Nutrition: Calories 138, total fat 23.2 g, carb 77 g, Protein 8.1 g, sodium 896 mg

Leek and Dijon Chicken

Preparation time: 15 minutes

Cooking time: 30 minutes

Servings: 4

Ingredients:

- 4 boneless skinless chicken breasts
- 1 tablespoon butter
- 1 cup leeks, sliced
- 1 tablespoon Dijon mustard
- 1 tablespoon water

Directions

1. Preheat oven to 200°F/93°C.

2. Add the butter to a large skillet and heat over medium heat. Add the chicken and brown evenly on all sides, approximately 7 minutes per side, depending upon thickness, until juices run clear.

3. Remove chicken from pan and place on an oven safe dish. Place in the oven to keep warm.

4. Add the leeks to the skillet that the chicken was cooked in and sauté over medium heat, stirring and scraping up any chicken residue that remained in the pan. Cook until soft and translucent, approximately 3-5 minutes.

5. In a small bowl, combine the Dijon mustard, and water. Mix well before adding to the pan with the leeks. Warm gently.

6. Remove chicken from the oven and place on serving plates. Top with warm leek and Dijon sauce before serving.

Nutrition:

Calories 231, total fat 12.2 g, carb 17 g, Protein 8.1 g, sodium 896 mg

Asian BBQ Chicken

Preparation time: 15 minutes

Cooking time: 15 minutes

Servings: 4

Ingredients:

- 1 pound boneless chicken breast, cut into tenders
- 2 tablespoons soy sauce
- 2 tablespoons honey
- 1 teaspoon sesame oil
- 1 tablespoon garlic chili paste

Directions

1. Begin by preparing and preheating the grill (either indoor or outdoor grill).

2. In a small bowl, combine the soy sauce, honey, sesame oil, and chili paste. Mix until well blended.

3. Take chicken tenders and gently slide them lengthwise onto metal or bamboo skewers.

4. Baste each skewer with the BBQ sauce.

5. Place skewers on a grill and cooks for approximately 10-15 minutes, turning once, until chicken juices run clear. Remove from heat and serve immediately.

Chicken Piccata

Preparation time: 5 minutes

Cooking time: 25 minutes

Servings: 4

Ingredients:

- 4 boneless, skinless chicken breasts
- ¼ cup butter
- 1 cup dry white wine
- ¼ cup lemon juice
- 3 tablespoons capers
- 1 teaspoon salt
- 1 teaspoon pepper

Directions

1. Preheat oven to 200°F/93°C.

2. Begin by gently pounding the chicken breasts until they are approximately ¼-inch thick. Season with salt and pepper.

3. Over medium-high heat, add the butter to a large sauté pan. Add the chicken and brown evenly on both sides, approximately 5-7 minutes per side, until juices run clear.

4. Transfer chicken, leaving remaining butter in the sauté pan, an oven-safe dish, and place in the oven to keep warm.

5. Add the dry white wine to the pan and reduce over medium heat for approximately 10 minutes, scraping the bottom of the pan occasionally to loosen any bits remaining from the chicken.

6. Add the lemon juice and capers. Cook for another 2 minutes.

7. Remove the chicken from the oven and place back in the pan. Heat through, spooning the sauce over the chicken for 1-2 minutes.

8. Transfer to serving plates and serve immediately.

Nutrition:

Calories 228, total fat 33.2 g, carb 17 g, Protein 8.1 g, sodium 896 mg

Sweet chicken surprise

Preparation time: 10 minutes

Cooking time: 40 minutes

Servings: 3

Ingredients:

- 2 x 200 g free-range chicken legs
- 1 bulb of garlic
- 250 g mixed-color seedless grapes
- 100 ml red vermouth
- Four sprigs of fresh tarragon

Directions:

1. Preheat the oven to 180ºC.

2. Put Dutch oven on high heat. Rub the chicken all over with a ½ t a tbsp. of butter, season with black pepper and salt with the skin side down in the Dutch oven.

3. Fry for few minutes until golden, then lightly squash the unpeeled garlic cloves with the heel of your hand and add. Pick in the grapes.

4. Turn the chicken skin side up, pour in the vermouth, transfer to the oven to roast for 40 minutes, or until the chicken is golden and tender. The sauce is sticky and reduced.

5. Add a little water to the pan and give it a gentle shimmy to pick up all the sticky bits. Pick over the tarragon, and dish up.

Preparation time: 10 minutes

Cooking time: 120 minutes

Servings: 3

Ingredients:

- 1 butternut squash (1.2kg)

- 100 g Thai red curry paste

- 1 x 1.6 kg whole free-range chicken

- 1 bunch of fresh coriander (30g)

- 1 x 400 milliliter tin of light coconut milk

Directions:

1. Sit in a big, deep pan with the chicken.

2. Carefully halve the length of the squash, then cut the seeds into 3 cm chunks.

3. Slice the stalks of coriander, add the squash, curry paste, and coconut milk to the Netherlands oven, and then pour 1 liter of water. Cover and cook for 1 hour and 20 minutes at medium heat.

4. Use tongs to remove a platter from the chicken. Sprinkle some fat on the chicken from the soup sheet, then sprinkle with half the leaves of coriander.

5. Serve at the table with 2 forks to split the meat. Crush some of the squash using a potato masher, giving a thicker texture to your soup.

6. Taste, season to perfection with black pepper and salt, then divide between six bowls and sprinkle with the remaining coriander.

7. Add chicken and Shred, as you dig in.

Nutrition:

Calories 118, total fat 15.2 g, carb 37 g, Protein 8.1 g, sodium 896 mg

Preparation time: 10 minutes

Cooking time: 5 hours

Servings: 3

Ingredients:

- 3-4 lb. whole frying chicken
- 1 tsp. poultry seasoning
- 1/4 tsp. basil

Directions:

1. Wash chicken and pat dry. Sprinkle cavity with poultry seasoning. Put in the Dutch oven and sprinkle with basil. Cover and bake for about 5 hours or until tender.

Easy Chicken Dinner

Preparation time: 10 minutes

Cooking time: 30 minutes

Servings: 3

Ingredients:

- 2 Chickens
- Carrots
- Seasonings
- Flour
- Potatoes

Directions:

1. Cut vegetables and potatoes for eating into small pieces. Split eight pieces of the chicken. Chicken of the back. In a plastic bag, mix the flour and seasonings. Put two pieces of chicken in the bag at a time and shake.

2. Once coated, remove the chicken from the bag and repeat until all the chicken has been eaten. Place and shake the potatoes in the bag. Cut from the bag the vegetables.

3. In the Dutch oven, add around 1/2 inches of oil and put on the coals. Add chicken and brown on all sides when the oil is hot. Drain excess oil from the pot and remove the chicken from the dish. Return the chicken to the bowl.

4. Apply around 1/4 inch warm water. Place over chicken potatoes and vegetables. Cover the pot and place it on the coals.

5. Set on top of the oven, ten coals. Cook until chicken is tender for 1 hour. Check regularly to ensure that a small amount of moisture is always present in the Netherlands oven.

Nutrition:

Calories 128, total fat 14.2 g, carb 47 g, Protein 18.1 g, sodium 596 mg

Preparation time: 10 minutes

Cooking time: 30 minutes

Servings: 3

Ingredients:

- 1 Whole chicken cooked, b1d, chopped
- 2 cans Cream of Chicken Soup or 1 can Golden Mushroom soup
- 1 c Mayonnaise
- 1 box "Stove Top" stuffing, chicken flavor
- Cheddar cheese

Directions:

1. Combine soup and mayonnaise in a massive bowl of choice. Then season pkg from stuffing mix and 3/4c stuffing crumbs.

2. Add chicken and mix well. Place in the Dutch oven, and then you top with remaining crumbs. Bake at 350 degrees Celsius for 30 min until bubbly and crumbs are brown. Variation change 1 can Golden Mushroom soup with Cream of Chicken soup. Add shredded cheddar cheese in the soup mixture, depending on your choice. You can sprinkle on it.

Nutrition:

Calories 318, total fat 23.2 g, carb 17 g, Protein 8.1 g, sodium 126 mg

Scrambled egg omelet

Preparation time: 10 minutes

Cooking time: 30 minutes

Servings: 3

Ingredients:

- 350 g ripe mixed-color tomatoes
- ½-1 fresh red chili
- ½ a bunch of fresh basil (15g)
- Four large free-range eggs
- ½ x 125 g ball of moz.zarella

Directions:

1. Slice the tomatoes thinly, place them on a sharing tray, then dress with a little extra virgin butter, red vinegar, sea salt, and black pepper.

2. Put most of the basil leaves into a pestle and mortar, pound into a paste with a pinch of salt, then muddle extra virgin butter in 1 tablespoon to make basil oil.

3. Slice the chili finely. Cut the mozzarella perfectly.

4. Put the Dutch oven with half a tablespoon of butter on medium heat. Beat and pour in the eggs, stir periodically with a rubber spatula, gently pushing the eggs around the Netherlands oven.

5. Stop the stir and scatter the mozzarella at the center when they are gently scrambled but still loose, then drizzle over the basil oil.

6. Let the bottom of the rest of the egg for 1 minute, then use the spatula to flip it back to the center, then fold the top half back over as well. Turn it to the tomato platter upside down, right side up.

7. Slice down the center to reveal in the middle the oozy scrambled eggs

Nutrition:

Calories 128, total fat 15.2 g, carb 37 g, Protein 5.1 g, sodium 506 mg

Vegetarian and Side Dish Recipes

Grilled Sweet Potato Fries

Preparation time: 10 minutes

Cooking time: 20 minutes

Servings: 3

Ingredients:

- 2 Medium Sweet Potatoes
- 2 Tablespoons Butter or Vegetable Oil
- 1 Clove of Garlic, Chopped
- 1 Teaspoon Chili Powder
- 1 A packet of Ranch Dry Mix

Directions

1. Wash the Sweet Potatoes and dry them. Then cut them in lengthwise strips, about 1/3 an inch wide on each side, so they look like fries.

2. The important thing is that they must be uniform so they can cook up at the same time. If you wanted to produce crispier fries and have the time, soak the chips in water for about 30 minutes and then let them drain for an hour before continuing. If otherwise, then that's fine too; they'll still be delicious.

3. Mix all the recipe ingredients in a bowl. We want all the beautiful spices and dry mix to be uniformly covered.

Place the Dutch oven on a grate over an open fire or on the middle rack of a grill.

4. We're going to cook the potatoes and make them soft and crispy on the outside. You want about ten minutes per side, depending on your heat flipping once.

Nutrition:

Calories 110, total fat 10.2 g, carb 37 g, Protein 8.1 g, sodium 236 mg

Blistered Shishito Peppers

Preparation time: 10 minutes

Cooking time: 20 minutes

Servings: 3

Ingredients

- 2 garlic cloves, sliced into chips
- 2 tablespoons oil
- 1 large shallot, thinly sliced

Directions:

1. Oil and garlic chips to a cold Dutch oven, and turn the heat on to medium. This will allow garlic to infuse the oil with flavor.

2. Observe the garlic chips, and remove them from the oil with a slotted spoon just when they begin to brown. It happens quickly, and they are easy to burn. Set aside.

3. Turn the heat up to medium-high, and add the peppers to the hot garlic oil. They will crackle and blister. Turn them occasionally until they are dried and blistered all over. You may have to remove smaller 1s before larger 1s.

4. Sprinkle the top with garlic chips, and either serve warm or pack in a jar for enjoying later.

Nutrition: Calories 128, total fat 12.2 g, carb 61 g, Protein 8.5 g, sodium 124 mg

Preparation time: 10 minutes

Cooking time: 35 minutes

Servings: 3

Ingredients:

- 1 small head of cabbage or 1/2 large head, chopped

- Five medium potatoes, sliced in bite-size wheels

- 1 or 2 Polish or Kielbasa type sausages (all kinds I tried were great, even bulk sausage!)

- 1 cup of water

- Butter

Directions:

1. Get 1 pot (Dutch oven), layer chopped cabbage, potatoes, sausage, and then repeat until all ingredients are used.

2. Add water and Butter, cover, and simmer until cabbage and potatoes, and sausages are cooked. Probably about 15 or 20 minutes.

Nutrition:

Calories 134, total fat 10.2 g, carb 47 g, Protein 13 g, sodium 226 mg

Sizzling seared scallops

Preparation time: 10 minutes

Cooking time: 20 minutes

Servings: 3

Ingredients:

- 200 g frozen peas
- 400 g potatoes
- ½ a bunch of fresh mint (15g)
- 6-8 raw king scallops (coral attached, trimmed, from sustainable sources)
- 50 g firm higher-welfare black pudding

Directions:

1. Wash the potatoes, chop into 3 cm chunks and cook for 1-2 minutes or until tender, adding the peas for the rest 3 minutes in the Dutch oven of boiling salted water.

2. Meanwhile, most of the mint leaves are picked and finely chopped and put aside.

3. Place 1 tablespoon of butter and leaves the remaining mint to crisp for 1 minute, then scoop the leaves onto a plate and leave the oil behind.

4. Season the scallops on each side for 2 minutes or until golden with sea salt and black pepper. Crumble it in the black pudding (so it chips next to each other).

5. Drain the potatoes and peas, return to the oven, properly mash with the chopped mint and 1 tablespoon of extra virgin butter, taste, and season.

6. Layer with the scallops and black pudding and sprinkle lightly with extra virgin butter.

Nutrition:

Calories 145, total fat 16 g, carb 35 g, Protein 8.1 g, sodium 812 mg

Pan Toasted Couscous

Preparation time: 5 minutes

Cooking time: 30 minutes

Servings: 4

Ingredients:

- 2 cups chicken stock
- 1¼ cup couscous
- 1 tablespoon butter
- ¼ cup shallots, diced
- 1 lemon, juiced, and zested

Directions

1. Add the chicken stock to a saucepan and bring to a boil over medium-high heat.

2. Add the couscous and stir. Remove from heat, cover, and let sit 5-7 minutes, or until all liquid has been absorbed.

3. In a large sauté pan, heat the butter over medium heat. Add the shallots and cook for 2 minutes. Add 1 tablespoon of lemon juice and two teaspoons of lemon zest. Stir and cook for 1 minute.

4. Add the couscous into the sauté pan and increase the heat to high. Cook, often stirring for 10 minutes. Reduce the heat to medium-low and cook, occasionally stirring for 20 minutes.

5. Remove from heat and serve immediately.

Nutrition: Calories 138, total fat 12.2 g, carb 52 g, Protein 10.1 g, sodium 124 mg

Fresh Cucumber Salad

Preparation time: 5 minutes

Cooking time: 0 minutes

Servings: 4

Ingredients:

- 3 cups cucumber, cubed
- 1½ cups watermelon, cut into small cubes
- ½ cup red onion, sliced
- ½ cup fresh cilantro, chopped
- 2 teaspoons fresh lime juice

Directions

1. In a large bowl, combine the cucumber, watermelon, and red onion.
2. Season with cilantro, lime juice, salt, and pepper. Mix well.
3. Place in the refrigerator and chill for at least 2 hours.
4. Stir well before serving.

Nutrition:

Calories 214, total fat 14 g, carb 17 g, Protein 4.1 g, sodium 456mg

Sweet Roasted Root Vegetables

Preparation time: 5 minutes

Cooking time: 30 minutes

Servings: 4

Ingredients:

- ¼ cup butter, melted
- 2 cups carrots, chopped
- 1 cup sweet potato, diced
- 1 cup rutabaga, diced
- ¼ cup wildflower honey

Directions

1. Preheat oven to 400°F/204°C.
2. In a bowl, combine the carrots, sweet potato, and rutabaga.
3. Drizzle the vegetables with melted butter and honey. Season with salt and pepper. Toss well to coat.
4. Spread the vegetables out on a baking sheet. Place in the oven and bake for 30-35 minutes, or until vegetables are tender and caramelized.

Nutrition:

Calories 138, total fat 12.2 g, carb 77 g, Protein 3 g, sodium 1122 mg

Fennel Gratin

Preparation time: 10 minutes

Cooking time: 60 minutes

Servings: 4

Ingredients:

- 3 cups fennel, sliced
- ¾ cup vegetable stock
- ¼ cup butter
- 1 cup fine bread crumbs
- 1 cup fresh grated parmesan cheese
- 1 teaspoon salt
- 1 teaspoon pepper

Directions

1. Preheat oven to 375°F/191°C.

2. Place the fennel slices in a lightly oiled 8"x8" baking dish. Cover with chicken stock and 2 tablespoons of butter cubed. Season with salt and pepper.

3. Cover and place in the oven—Bake for 35 minutes.

4. Meanwhile, in a small saucepan, melt the remaining butter. Add in the breadcrumbs, parmesan cheese, and additional salt and pepper, if desired.

5. Removed gratin from the oven and top with bread crumb mixture.

6. Recover the dish and place back in the oven. Bake for an additional 30-35 minutes, or until the fennel is tender.

7. Let rest 5 minutes before serving.

Nutrition:

Calories 328, total fat 12 g, carb 30g, Protein 9 g, sodium 126 mg

Preparation time: 5 minutes

Cooking time: 30 minutes

Servings: 4

Ingredients:

- 1 tablespoon butter
- 4 cups fresh corn kernels
- 2½ cups milk
- 1 cup Monterey Jack cheese, shredded

Directions

1. In a Dutch oven, melt the butter over medium heat. Add the corn kernels and cook while stirring for approximately 3-4 minutes, or until corn is slightly toasted.

2. Add the milk and bring the mixture to a boil over medium-high heat for two minutes. Season with salt and pepper.

3. Transfer one half of the soup to a blender and pulse until creamy and thick. Return to the Dutch oven and mix well.

4. Gently reheat soup over low heat.

5. Serve immediately topped with Monterey jack cheese.

Nutrition: Calories 248, total fat 19.2g, carb 10g, Protein 8.1 g, sodium 196 mg

Pita Pizza Blanco

Preparation time: 10 minutes

Cooking time: 15 minutes

Servings: 4

Ingredients:

- 4 pieces of pita bread
- ¾ cup crème Fraiche
- 3 cloves garlic, crushed and minced
- ½ cup fresh oregano, chopped
- 1½ cup fresh mozzarella cheese, sliced

Directions

1. Preheat oven to 420°F/216°C.
2. Spread out the pita bread pieces on one or two baking sheets.
3. In a bowl, combine the crème fraiche, garlic, and oregano. Blend well.
4. Spread the mixture evenly on each of the pita breads. Top with several slices of fresh mozzarella cheese.
5. Place in the oven and bake for 15 minutes, or until cheese is golden and bubbly.
6. Serve warm.

Nutrition: Calories 198, total fat 23.2 g, carb 37 g, Protein 6.1 g, sodium 126 mg

Ancient Grain Stuffed Peppers

Preparation time: 5 minutes

Cooking time: 35 minutes

Servings: 4

Ingredients:

- 4 large red bell peppers, tops removed and seeds scooped out
- 3 cups ancient grain blend, cooked
- 1 tablespoon butter
- 2 cups white mushrooms, sliced
- ½ cup fresh parsley, chopped

Directions

1. Preheat oven to 350°F/177°C.
2. In a large bowl combine the ancient grains, butter, mushrooms, and parsley. Season with salt and pepper as desired.
3. Stuff each pepper liberally with the mixture and replace the tops of the peppers.
4. Transfer the peppers to a baking dish and add 1 tablespoon of water to the dish's bottom.
5. Place in the oven and bake for 35-40 minutes, or until peppers are tender.
6. Serve immediately.

Nutrition: Calories 167, total fat 15 g, carb 73 g, Protein 13 g, sodium 436 mg

Parmesan Risotto

Preparation time: 10 minutes

Cooking time: 35 minutes

Servings: 4

Ingredients:

- 1 large shallot, finely chopped

- 2 quarts low-sodium vegetable or chicken broth, at room temperature

- 2 cups Arborio, carnaroli, or vialone nano rice

- ½ cup dry white wine

- 1 cup Parmesan cheese, finely grated

Directions

1. Add the butter to the Dutch oven and melt it over medium-high heat.

2. Mix in the rice until mixed well with the butter. Stir-cook for about 2 minutes until lightly toasted and aromatic.

3. Mix in the wine and simmer for 3 minutes until the wine is almost completely reduced and nearly dry.

4. Pour in the broth ½ cup at a time, stirring with each addition.

5. Cook for 20–30 minutes until the mixture is thickened and the rice is al dente.

6. Add some more butter and cheese, if desired.

7. Serve warm.

Nutrition

Calories 165, Fat 11 g, carbs 66 g, Protein 20 g, sodium 120 mg

Preparation time: 5 minutes

Cooking time: 35 minutes

Servings: 4

Ingredients:

- 3 cups of water

- 3½ cups whole milk

- 1 pound elbow macaroni

- 4 ounces Velveeta, cubed

- 2 cups sharp cheddar, shredded

Directions

1. Add the water, milk, and pasta to the Dutch oven. Stir and heat over medium-high heat.

2. Reduce heat to medium-low and simmer, stirring occasionally, for 12–15 minutes until the mixture is thickened and the pasta is tender.

3. Mix in the Velveeta and cheese and simmer over low heat until melted.

4. Serve warm.

Nutrition

Calories 344, Fat 14 g, carbs 39 g, Protein 16 g, sodium 450 mg

Creamy Mushroom Pasta

Preparation time: 5 minutes

Cooking time: 15 minutes

Servings: 4

Ingredients:

- 2 tablespoons butter
- ¾ pound mixed mushrooms (shiitake, cremini, oyster, etc.), sliced
- 3 cloves garlic, minced
- 1-quart chicken, mushroom, or vegetable broth
- Grated Parmesan cheese

Directions

1. Add the oil to the Dutch oven and heat it over medium-high heat.
2. Add the mushrooms and stir cook for about 4 minutes until lightly browned.
3. Add the garlic, cream, pasta, and broth and stir-cook for a few seconds.
4. Bring to a boil, and then reduce heat to low and simmer for about 12 minutes, occasionally stirring, until the pasta is cooked well and the mixture is thickened.
5. Serve warm with thyme and grated Parmesan on top.

Nutrition : Calories 607, Fat 26 g, carbs 71 g, Protein 20 g, sodium 1050 mg

Mascarpone Pumpkin Pasta

Preparation time: 5 minutes

Cooking time: 15 minutes

Servings: 4

Ingredients:

- 1 cup canned pumpkin puree
- 1-quart vegetable broth
- 1 cup of water
- ¾ pound dry penne pasta
- 2 teaspoons fresh rosemary leaves, finely chopped

Directions

1. Add the pumpkin puree, broth, water, and pasta to the Dutch oven and bring to a boil over medium-high heat.

2. Reduce heat to low and simmer for 10–12 minutes until most of the liquid evaporates, stirring occasionally.

3. Mix in the mascarpone, rosemary

4. Stir-cook for about 2 minutes until the pasta is cooked to your satisfaction.

5. Serve warm with grated Parmesan on top.

Nutrition

Calories 245, Fat 4 g, carbs 43g, Protein 8 g, sodium 63 mg

Classic Cheesy Spaghetti

Preparation time: 10 minutes

Cooking time: 12 minutes

Servings: 4

Ingredients:

- ½ cup of water
- 1-quart chicken broth
- ¾ pound dry spaghetti
- 1 Parmesan cheese rind (optional)
- ¾ cup Pecorino-Romano cheese, grated

Directions

1. Add the water, broth, and pasta and Parmesan rind to the Dutch oven and bring to a boil over medium-high heat.
2. Simmer for 8–9 minutes until most of the liquid evaporates, stirring occasionally.
3. Mix in the Pecorino-Romano
4. Stir-cook for 2 minutes until the pasta is cooked to your satisfaction.
5. Remove the Parmesan rind.
6. Serve warm.

Nutrition*:* Calories 497, Fat 10.5 g, carbs 73.5 g, Protein 25 g, sodium 685 mg

Braised Leeks

Preparation time: 15 minutes

Cooking time: 50 minutes

Servings: 4

Ingredients:

- 6 medium leeks (white portion and light green parts only), halved lengthwise
- ¼ cup butter
- 1 teaspoon dry rosemary (or 2 teaspoons fresh rosemary)
- 2 teaspoons sugar
- ½ cup dry white wine

Directions

1. Preheat the oven 350ºF (180°C).
2. Clean the leeks under cold running water to remove any remaining dirt.
3. Add the butter in the Dutch oven, and let melt over medium-low heat. Add the leeks and brown them on the cut side down for 2-3 minutes over medium heat.
4. Turn the leeks over, add the remaining ingredients. Stir to combine. Cover and place in the oven. Bake for 35-45 minutes checking midway to turn over the leeks back cut side down. Add a bit of water if needed to prevent the leeks from sticking to the bottom.

5. Remove from the oven once the leeks are tender. If there is lots of cooking juice, you can reduce it on the stove, uncovered, over medium-high heat until most of the liquid has evaporated.

Nutrition

Calories 153, Fat 5 g, carbs 18 g, Protein 3 g, sodium 77 mg

French Onion Pasta

Preparation time: 10 minutes

Cooking time: 35 minutes

Servings: 4

Ingredients:

- 3 tablespoons butter
- 1½ pounds yellow onions, sliced paper-thin
- ⅔ Cup water
- 1-quart low-sodium vegetable or beef broth
- ¾ pound dry orecchiette pasta
- ⅓ cup ruby port
- 2 ounces (about ¾ cup) Gruyere cheese, finely shredded
- Salt and pepper to taste

Directions

1. Add the oil to the Dutch oven and heat it over medium-high heat.
2. Add the onion slices and stir-cook for 15–20 minutes until caramelized and dark.
3. Add the water, broth, pasta, and ruby port; stir and cook for 12 minutes until the liquid is evaporated.
4. Mix in the Gruyere. Season to taste with salt and pepper.
5. Serve warm.

Nutrition

Calories 520, Fat 12 g, carbs 84 g, Protein 17.5 g, sodium 1259 mg

Seasoned French Fries

Preparation time: 5 minutes

Cooking time: 60 minutes

Servings: 4

Ingredients:

- 3 pounds russet potatoes, cut into ½-inch sticks
- 3 quarts peanut oil
- 2 teaspoons Old Bay seasoning

Directions

1. Add the potato sticks to a bowl and cover with cold water; set aside for 30–60 minutes. Drain and pat dry.

2. Add the peanut oil to the Dutch oven and heat it to 325°F (160°C).

3. In 2–3 batches, fry the potato sticks for 7–9 minutes until golden brown.

4. Drain over paper towels.

5. Increase heat to 400°F (200°C).

6. Return the cooked potato sticks to the Dutch oven in 2–3 batches and fry for 1–2 minutes until deep golden brown.

7. Drain over paper towels.

8. Serve warm.

Nutrition: Calories 226, Fat 7 g, carbs 39 g, Protein 5 g, sodium 397 mg

Preparation time: 10 minutes

Cooking time: 10 minutes

Servings: 4

Ingredients:

- 1 cup of water
- 2 pounds carrots cut into 2-inch pieces
- ⅓ Cup butter
- 2 tablespoons all-purpose flour
- 2 teaspoons chicken bouillon granules

Directions

1. Pour 1 inch of water into the Dutch oven.
2. Add the carrots and boil for 6–8 minutes until tender. Drain and set aside.
3. Add the butter and melt it over medium-high heat.
4. Add the onion and stir-cook until softened and translucent.
5. Add the flour and bouillon
6. Bring to a boil and then simmer for about 2 minutes until the mixture is thickened, stirring occasionally.
7. Stir in the carrots.

Nutrition: Calories 129, Fat 8 g, carbs 14 g, Protein 2 g, sodium 416 mg

Baked Garlic and Mushroom Rice

Preparation time: 10 minutes

Cooking time: 40 minutes

Servings: 4

Ingredients:

- 3 tablespoons butter
- 1 pound mushrooms, diced
- 3 cloves garlic, minced
- 1½ cups of rice
- ½ cup white wine

Directions

1. Warm the butter in the Dutch oven over medium heat.
2. Stir in the diced mushrooms and minced garlic.
3. Cook for about 10 minutes and then stir in the rice.
4. Pour in the white wine and cook for 2 minutes. Pour in the water, bring to a boil, and cover.
5. Bake at 350°F (180°C) for about 25 minutes.
6. Remove the lid and cook uncovered for 5 minutes until the rice is set and nicely baked.

Nutrition

Calories 406, Fat 11.3 g, carbs 63.3 g, Protein 9 g, sodium 18 mg

Quinoa with Mixed Vegetables and Artichoke Hearts

Preparation time: 5 minutes

Cooking time: 40 minutes

Servings: 4

Ingredients:

- 3 tablespoons butter
- 2 cloves garlic, minced
- 1 (14-ounce) bag of frozen vegetables
- ½ cup artichoke hearts, diced
- 2 cups quinoa, washed and rinsed

Directions

1. Warm the butter in the Dutch oven over medium heat.
2. Stir in the minced garlic, frozen veggies, and diced artichoke hearts.
3. Cook for 5 minutes and then stir in the quinoa.
4. Pour in the water and bring to a simmer.
5. Reduce heat to low, cover, and cook for 20 minutes.
6. Remove the lid and mix everything to fluff up the quinoa with the veggies.
7. Serve on plates.

Nutrition: Calories 490, Fat 15.9 g, carbs 72.8 g, Protein 15.9 g, sodium 67 mg

Dutch Oven Vegetarian Lasagna

Preparation time: 5 minutes

Cooking time: 40 minutes

Servings: 4

Ingredients:

- 5 tablespoons butter
- 4 cups baby spinach
- ½ pound lasagna sheets
- 1 (28-ounce) can tomato sauce
- 4 cups grated mozzarella cheese

Directions

1. Warm the butter in the Dutch oven over medium heat.

2. Stir in the baby spinach

3. Cook for 5 minutes until the spinach wilts.

4. Stir in the tomato sauce and cook for 5 minutes.

5. Remove from heat and transfer all but a little of the filling to a bowl.

6. Add a layer of lasagna sheets to the Dutch oven. Add a layer of the filling and sprinkle with mozzarella cheese.

7. Repeat at least two more times or until you run out of lasagna sheets and filling. Sprinkle the top with mozzarella cheese and pepper.

8. Cover and bake at 350°F (180°C) for about 20 minutes.

9. Remove the lid and cook uncovered for about 15 more minutes until the mozzarella is golden brown.

10. Let cool slightly, then slice and serve.

Nutrition

Calories 490, Fat 24 g, carbs 54.6 g, Protein 19.3 g, sodium 1238 mg

Cheesy Ravioli Pasta Bake

Preparation time: 5 minutes

Cooking time: 40 minutes

Servings: 4

Ingredients:

- 3 tablespoons butter
- 1 pound mushrooms, diced
- 4 (9-ounce) packages of spinach ravioli
- 1 (24-ounce) jar marinara sauce
- ½ pound mozzarella cheese, shredded

Directions

1. Warm the butter in the Dutch oven over medium heat. Add the diced mushrooms.
2. Stir in the marinara sauce.
3. Let the flavors marry together, and then add the ravioli.
4. Bring to simmer and transfer the Dutch oven to a preheated oven at 350°F (180°C).
5. Bake for 25–30 minutes.

Nutrition

Calories 747, Fat 37.4 g, carbs 69.3 g, Protein 36.1 g, sodium 2030 mg

Vegetarian Jambalaya

Preparation time: 5 minutes

Cooking time: 35 minutes

Servings: 4

Ingredients:

- 2 tablespoons butter
- 1 (14-ounce) bag of frozen vegetables
- 2 (16-ounce) cans red beans, drained and rinsed
- 1 cup long-grain rice
- 1 (28-ounce) can diced tomatoes

Directions

1. Warm the butter in the Dutch oven over medium heat.
2. Stir in the frozen veggies and cook for 5–7 minutes.
3. Stir in the rice and cook for 2–3 minutes.
4. Stir in the diced tomatoes and water.
5. Mix and bring to a boil.
6. Reduce heat to low and simmer, covered, for 20 minutes.
7. Stir in the red beans and serve warm.

Nutrition

Calories 1113, Fat 9.9 g, carbs 202.2 g, Protein 59.4 g, sodium 489 mg

Stuffed Zucchini

Preparation time: 20 minutes

Cooking time: 40 minutes

Servings: 5

Ingredients:

- 2 tablespoons butter
- 2 large onions, chopped
- 1 cup quinoa, rinsed
- 1 cup cannellini beans, drained
- ½ cup almonds, chopped

Directions

1. Place a cast-iron Dutch oven over the campfire or hot coals.

2. Heat the oil and sauté the onions.

3. Add the quinoa and water.

4. Bring the mixture to a boil, put on the lid, and let it cook for 10 minutes.

5. Transfer this cooked quinoa to a bowl, and add the beans and almonds.

6. Cut the zucchini lengthwise, and scoop out the seeds.

7. Fill the zucchinis with the quinoa stuffing.

8. Wipe out the Dutch oven with a paper towel, and spray it with cooking spray.

9. Arrange the zucchinis in the Dutch oven. Cover, and place it over the heat.

10. If you're using charcoal, then put some coals on the lid.

11. Cook it for about 25–30 minutes.

12. When the zucchinis are fork-tender, serve.

Nutrition

Calories 407, total fat 13.2 g, Carb 58 g, Protein 18.5 g, sodium 34 mg

Meat Recipe

Country Style Ribs

Preparation Time: 10 minutes plus 24 hours marinating time

Cooking Time: 35 minutes

Servings: 6

Ingredients

- 6 pounds country-style pork ribs
- Barbecue sauce, for basting
- Marinade
- 3 tablespoons olive oil
- ⅓ cup hoisin sauce
- ⅓ cup soy sauce
- 4 teaspoons minced ginger
- ¾ cup whisky
- Zest of one orange
- Juice of one orange
- ½ cup light brown sugar
- 6 cloves garlic, minced
- 2 cups barbeque sauce

Directions

1. Place ribs in a large pot or Dutch oven and cover with water. Bring to a boil and continue until partly cooked (about 20 minutes). Drain well.

2. Combine ingredients for the marinade.

3. Place ribs with the marinade in a shallow container with a lid or a large Ziploc bag.

4. Let marinate, refrigerated, for 24 hours to 2 days.

5. Bring to room temperature before grilling.

6. Grill over medium heat for about 15 minutes, flipping frequently and basting with barbecue sauce.

Nutrition

Calories 985 Carbs 23.5 g Fat 56 g Protein 94.1 g Sodium 1025 mg

Camper's Beer Braised Short Ribs

Preparation Time: 10 minutes

Cooking Time: Slow Cooker: 8 hours; Dutch Oven: 2 hours

Servings: 3–4

Ingredients

- 3 pounds beef short ribs, bone-in
- 3 medium onions, cut into wedges
- 1 bay leaf

Sauce

- 1 (12-ounce) bottle beer
- 2 tablespoons brown sugar
- 2 tablespoons Dijon mustard
- 2 tablespoons tomato paste
- 2 teaspoons dried thyme
- 2 teaspoons beef bouillon granules
- 1 teaspoon salt
- ¼ teaspoon pepper

Slurry (optional)

- 3 tablespoons all-purpose flour
- ½ cup cold water

Directions

1. Slow Cooker: Place ribs, onions, and bay leaf in a slow cooker. Combine sauce ingredients and add to ribs. Cover and cook for 8 hours on Low. Transfer ribs and onions to

a bowl or wrap in foil and set aside. Heat the remaining juices in a saucepan over medium heat until reduced and thickened. If desired, mix slurry ingredients in a small bowl and stir into juices for a thicker sauce. Spoon over ribs and serve.

2. Dutch Oven: Arrange coals in a ring (about 7 briquettes) in the cooking pit, leaving a space at the center. Place ribs, onions, and bay leaf in the Dutch oven. Mix sauce ingredients together and pour over ribs. Cover and place briquettes (about 13) in a ring on the lid. Rotate lid every 30 minutes for even cooking and replace briquettes as needed. Cook until ribs can be pierced easily and flesh pulls away from the bone at the ends (internal temperature: 180–190°F). Transfer ribs and onions to a bowl or wrap in foil and set aside. Heat the remaining juices until reduced and thickened. If desired, mix slurry ingredients in a small bowl and stir into juices for a thicker sauce. Spoon over ribs and serve.

Nutrition

Calories 418 Carbs 22 g Fat 19 g Protein 46 g Sodium 821 mg

Preparation Time: 10 minutes

Cooking Time: 10 minutes

Servings: 2–4

Ingredients

- 1 pound ground beef
- 1 packet taco seasoning mix
- 1 medium tomato, chopped
- ¼ head lettuce, shredded
- 1 small onion, chopped
- 1 cup shredded cheese of choice (like cheddar or Monterey)
- ½ cup sour cream
- ¼ cup taco sauce
- 2–4 individual bags of corn chips, opened neatly on top

Directions

1. Brown beef over medium heat in a nonstick pan or cast-iron skillet.

2. Add seasoning and cook according to package instructions.

3. Divide into 2–4, depending on the number of packets.

4. Add to packets of corn chips.

5. Add other ingredients as desired.

6. Stir with a fork and eat directly from the packets.

Nutrition: Calories 653 Carbs 23.4 g Fat 48.6 g Protein 31 g Sodium 558 mg

Tinfoil Sausage & Veggies

Preparation Time: 15 minutes

Cooking Time: 10–20 minutes

Servings: 4–6

Ingredients

- 1 red bell pepper, seeded and sliced thinly
- 2 ears shucked corn, cut into 1-inch disks
- 1 medium onion, chopped
- 4–5 small red potatoes cut into bite-size pieces
- 1 medium-sized zucchini, sliced
- 1 (13-ounce) package smoked turkey sausage, sliced
- Parsley, chopped, for sprinkling

Seasoning

- 5 tablespoons olive oil
- 1 tablespoon dried oregano
- 1 tablespoon dried parsley flakes
- ½ teaspoon garlic powder
- 1 teaspoon paprika
- Salt and pepper, to taste

Directions

1. Mix seasoning ingredients together in a large bowl.

2. Add bell pepper, corn, onion, potatoes, zucchini, and sausage. Toss to coat with seasoning.

3. For one serving, stack two sheets of foil together or use one sheet of heavy-duty aluminum foil. Place about a fourth of the seasoned veggie-and-sausage mix at the center of the foil. Fold over and seal. Repeat with remaining ingredients.

4. Place on preheated grill and cook until veggies are crisp-tender (about 10–20 minutes).

5. Remove from heat and serve sprinkled with chopped parsley.

Nutrition: Calories 333 Carbs 31.2 g Fat 17.1 g Protein 16 g Sodium 398 mg \

Foil Hamburgers

Preparation Time: 15 minutes

Cooking Time: 30–40 minutes

Servings: 4

Ingredients

8 small new potatoes, unpeeled, quartered

1 teaspoon seasoned salt, or to taste

1 teaspoon Italian seasoning, or to taste

4 (¼-pound) frozen hamburger patties

1 cup frozen cut green beans

1 tablespoon olive oil

Directions

1. Stack 2 aluminum foil sheets on top of each other (or use one sheet of heavy-duty foil). Place one patty, ¼ of potatoes, and ¼ of green beans on the center of the stacked sheets. Sprinkle with about ¼ teaspoon each seasoned salt, Italian seasoning (or to taste), and olive oil. Fold sides of the foil over, leaving room for steam, and seal securely. Repeat for remaining ingredients.

2. Place on preheated grill at medium heat and cover. Let cook until patties are done (internal temperature: 160°F) and vegetables are tender (about 30–40 minutes), flipping the packets over midway through cooking.

3. Open carefully to release steam and serve.

Nutrition: Calories 410 Carbs 41 g Fat 16 g Protein 25 g Sodium 420 mg

A meal in a Can

Preparation Time: 5 minutes

Cooking Time: 35–45 minutes

Servings: 1

Ingredients

- 1 (about ¼-pound) hamburger patty
- 1 small red potato, quartered
- ⅓ medium carrot, peeled and cut into chunks
- 1 tablespoon chopped onion
- ½ small Roma tomato
- 2 tablespoons corn kernels
- 1 tablespoon butter or olive oil
- Salt and pepper, to taste

Directions

1. Layer the ingredients as listed in a clean coffee can.

2. Cover tightly with foil. This may be kept in a cooler until the campfire or grill is ready.

3. Place on a grate over the campfire or coals at about medium heat.

4. Let cook until potatoes are done (about 35–45 minutes).

Nutrition

Calories 556 Carbs 36.1 g Fat 34.8 g Protein 23.3 g Sodium 571 mg

Beef & Potato Packets

Preparation time: 30 minutes

Cooking time: 25 minutes

Servings: 5

Ingredients:

- 1 tablespoon butter
- 2 tablespoons sherry vinegar
- 1 medium sweet potato, peeled and thinly sliced
- ½ cup onion, sliced
- 4 (6 ounces) servings of beef steak, trimmed of fat

Directions

1. Combine the oil, sherry vinegar, sweet potato, and onion in a bowl. Let it sit for few minutes.

2. Layout four double-layer sheets of foil, and coat the foil with cooking spray.

3. Using a slotted spoon, remove the vegetables from the sauce, and arrange them on the four foil pieces.

4. Place the meat in the sauce, and turn it to coat.

5. Top each serving with a piece of steak, and pour the sauce over.

6. Seal the packets, and place them on the grill.

7. Cook for 25 minutes, turning halfway.

8. Check that the steak is cooked to your liking and serve.

Nutrition: Calories 566, total fat 41 g, Carb 12.7 g, Protein 34.2 g, sodium 165 mg

Preparation time: 10 minutes

Cooking time: 20 minutes

Servings: 3

Ingredients:

- 3-4 lb. beef brisket
- 2-3 tbsp.. flour
- Seas1d tenderizer

Directions

1. Tenderizer coat brisket well. Wrap with 2 heavy-duty foil covers. Chill overnight. Cover and cook 225 to 250 for about 7 hours in the Dutch oven. You can cook it more quickly, but it's slowly cooked juicier.

2. Remove the foil and put it on a warm serving plate. Create a thin gravy with milk, rice. Before serving, pour over the brisket.

Nutrition:

Calories 408, total fat 11.2 g, carb 12 g, Protein 12.1 g, sodium 806 mg

Beef and Vegetable Stir Fry

Preparation time: 10 minutes

Cooking time: 35 minutes

Servings: 3

Ingredients:

- 1 tablespoon butter
- 1 (16-ounce) package frozen mixed vegetables
- 1 cup stir fry sauce
- 2 teaspoons cornstarch
- 2 cups cubed cooked roast beef

Directions:

1. Get your oven in the Netherlands, heat the oil. Remove the frozen vegetables and remove some water when the oil is hot, then stir—cover and cook for 3 minutes over medium heat.

2. In a small bowl, mix the stir fry sauce with the cornstarch. Pour the vegetables into the Netherlands oven and mix. Then add and stir the cooked beef.

3. Replace the cover, cook the beef and vegetables at low heat for 5 to 8 minutes, occasionally stirring, till the meat is tender, while the vegetables are still crisp.

Nutrition: Calories 178, total fat 14.2 g, carb 17 g, Protein 12.1 g, sodium 126 mg

Preparation time: 10 minutes

Cooking time: 6 hours

Servings: 3

Ingredients:

- 3 pounds short ribs
- 7 cloves garlic, crushed
- 2 cups tomato sauce (fresh or canned)
- ¾ cup balsamic vinegar
- 1 cup fresh figs, chopped

Directions

1. Take crushed garlic cloves and rub briskly over the short ribs. Cut the ribs and place them, along with any remaining garlic pieces, into a slow cooker.

2. In a small bowl, combine the tomato sauce, balsamic vinegar, and figs. Pour over the ribs and toss to coat.

3. Cook over low heat for 6-8 hours until ribs are fall off the bone tender.

Nutrition:

Calories 178, total fat 23 g, carb 12 g, Protein 9.1 g, sodium 126 mg

Grandma's Weekend Roast

Preparation time: 10 minutes

Cooking time: 125 minutes

Servings: 3

Ingredients:

- 1 4-pound beef roast
- ¼ cup butter
- 3 cups yellow onion, sliced
- 3 cups beef stock
- 1 cup red wine

Directions

1. Preheat oven to 325°F/163°C

2. Heat the butter in a Dutch oven over medium to medium-high heat.

3. Add the roast to the Dutch oven and brown evenly, approximately 3-5 minutes, on each side.

4. Remove meat from pan and temporarily set aside.

5. Add the onions to the pan, and cook until slightly soft, approximately 5 minutes.

6. Stir in the beef stock and red wine, and cook while stirring for 5-7 minutes. Season with additional salt and pepper, if desired.

7. Add the roast back into the Dutch oven, cover, and place in the oven. Cook for 2 hours, turn roast and then cook an additional 45 minutes.

8. Let roast rest 10 minutes before serving. Serve dressed with tender onions and pan sauce.

Nutrition:

Calories 147, total fat 12.2 g, carb 47 g, Protein 5.1 g, sodium 106 mg

Preparation time: 10 minutes

Cooking time: 65 minutes

Servings: 3

Ingredients:

- 1 2-pound flank steak, trimmed
- 1 tablespoon butter
- 3 cups fresh spinach, chopped
- 2 cups tomatoes, chopped
- 2 tablespoons prepared horseradish

Directions

1. Preheat oven to 425°F/218°C

2. Heat the butter over medium heat in a sauté pan. Add the spinach and tomatoes. Cook until spinach is wilted and tomatoes have begun to release a good amount of juice, approximately 4-5 minutes. Remove from heat.

3. Add one tablespoon of the horseradish to the spinach mixture. Mix well and set aside. Using a mallet, pound steak until it is approximately ¼-inch thick.

4. Take any butter that remains in the sauté pan and drizzle over the steak. Season with the remaining horseradish, salt, and pepper. Rub the mixture into the steak before turning the meat over.

5. Spread the spinach mixture along the steak. Starting at one end, begin rolling the steak lengthwise to create a

pinwheel. Secure the pinwheel with several pieces of chef's twine.Place the roll into a baking pan and bake for 45-50 minutes.

6. Let rest for 10 minutes before removing twine and slicing into pieces 1½-inch thick for serving.

Nutrition: Calories 343, total fat 12.2 g, carb 77 g, Protein 32.1 g, sodium 136 mg

Preparation time: 10 minutes

Cooking time: 45 minutes

Servings: 3

Ingredients:

- 2 pounds thin beef steak
- ¼ cup fresh cilantro
- 1 lime, quartered
- 1 tablespoon butter

Directions

1. Preheat oven to 350°F/177°C

2. Take one 18"x18" or larger piece of aluminum foil and lay it on a baking sheet.

3. Drizzle the foil with butter.

4. Cut the steak into four sections. Place steaks in the center portion of the foil.

5. Place jalapeños over the steaks and top with fresh cilantro and lime wedges.

6. Fold over the foil, creating a snug but not overly tight pouch around the meat, taking care to make sure that it is well sealed to avoid any juices escaping during cooking.

7. Place in the oven and cook for 35-40 minutes, or until steak has reached desired doneness.

8. Let rest 5-10 minutes before serving.

Nutrition:

Calories 138, total fat 13.2 g, carb 77 g, Protein 8.1 g, sodium 126 mg

Preparation time: 10 minutes

Cooking time: 45 minutes

Servings: 3

Ingredients:

- 1 pound beef steak
- 4 cups baby spinach, torn
- 2 cups beets, cut into small cubes
- ¼ cup shallots, sliced
- ¼ cup butter

Directions

1. Preheat oven to 400°F/204°C

2. Place the beet cubes on a baking sheet and drizzle with 2 tablespoons of the butter. Place in the oven and roast for 25-30 minutes, or until beets are caramelized and slightly crispy.

3. Add enough oil to a skillet to coat the bottom surface and heat over medium-high.

4. Season the steak liberally with salt and pepper. Pan sear the steak evenly on all sides for approximately 7 minutes for a one-inch steak. This time may vary depending upon the thickness and desired doneness.

5. Remove the steak from the heat and set it aside on a plate to rest.

6. Add the rest of the oil to the pan. Heat over medium.

7. Add the shallots to the pan and sauté until translucent, approximately 3-5 minutes.

8. Remove the beets from the oven and add them to the skillet. Toss while cooking for 3 minutes, or just long enough to crisp the beets' outsides just slightly.

9. Place the spinach in a serving bowl. Add the beets and shallots, along with a little of the butter and steak drippings, if desired. Toss gently.

10. Slice the steak and top the salad with the steak right before serving.

Nutrition:

Calories 321, total fat 13.2 g, carb 12 g, Protein 11 g, sodium 756 mg

Ginger Spiced Beef

Preparation time: 10 minutes

Cooking time: 35 minutes

Servings: 3

Ingredients:

- 1 pound flank steak, sliced into ½-inch strips
- ½ cup cornstarch
- 1 tablespoon sesame oil
- ¼ cup fresh grated ginger
- 1 medium orange, juiced, and zested

Directions

1. Mix cornstarch and water in bowl. Whisk until smooth and free of any lumps.

2. Heat the sesame oil over medium in a large sauté pan. Add the ginger to the oil and cook for 1 minute, or until fragrant.

3. Dip each strip of steak into the cornstarch mixture and place into the pan. Cook while tossing gently for 5-7 minutes.

4. Add ¼ cup fresh orange juice and 1 tablespoon orange zest. Cook while stirring for an additional 3-5 minutes, or until steak is cooked through.

5. Remove from heat and serve with rice, if desired.

Nutrition: Calories 143, total fat 15 g, carb 13 g, Protein 12 g, sodium 256 m

Soup and Stew

Camper's Onion Soup in Foil

Preparation Time: 5 minutes

Cooking Time: 40–60 minutes

Serving: 1

Ingredients

- 1 large onion
- 1 beef bouillon cube, crumbled
- 1–2 tablespoons softened or melted butter
- Dash of black pepper (optional)
- Grated Parmesan and/or Swiss cheese for sprinkling
- 1 slice baguette or any bread of choice, toasted

Directions

1. Butter one side of a thick sheet of aluminum (large enough to cover the whole onion, plus extra for twisting to seal and to serve as a 'tail' for easy handling).

2. Peel the onion and core like an apple, but not to the bottom; leave a 'well' at the center.

3. Fill the well with crumbled bouillon and butter.

4. Fold the aluminum over the onion and twist the ends to seal.

5. Place in coals, over the grill, or around campfire edges (find a place where heat is moderate and relatively even).

6. Cook until tender or easy to squeeze with tongs (about 40–60 minutes).

7. Place in a bowl and open the foil. Sprinkle with black pepper and cheese.

8. Serve with a baguette slice.

Nutrition

Calories 299 Carbs 25.9 g Fat 19.6 g Protein 6.1 gSodium 1152 mg

Easiest Beef Stew

Preparation Time: 2 minutes

Cooking Time: 10 minutes

Serving: 4

Ingredients

1 pound lean ground beef

1 (15-ounce) can of mixed vegetables

2 (11½-ounce) cans V–8 vegetable juice or tomato juice

Directions

1. Cook the ground beef in a Dutch oven in its juices until evenly browned (about 8–10 minutes).

2. Drain off any juices.

3. Add the rest of the ingredients.

4. Bring to a boil.

5. Reduce heat and let simmer until all the vegetables are heated through.

Nutrition

Calories 386 Carbs 16.8 g Fat 23.7 g Protein 23.8 g Sodium 537 mg

Corn and Sweet Potato Chowder

Preparation Time: 10 minutes

Cooking Time: 20 minutes

Servings: 4

Ingredients

- 4 bacon strips, chopped
- 1 medium onion, diced
- 2 (11-ounce) cans whole kernel corn, liquid drained into a separate container
- 2 cups water
- 1 (14.75-ounce) can cream of corn
- 4 medium-sized sweet potatoes, peeled and diced
- Salt and pepper, to taste

Directions

1. Cook the bacon in a deep pot until crisp. Optional: Scoop or drain out rendered fat as desired, leaving just enough to sauté onion.

2. Add onion and sauté until transparent (about 3–5 minutes).

3. Pour in water and corn liquid.

4. Bring to a boil.

5. Add sweet potatoes and cook until tender (about 5 minutes).

6. Stir in kernels and cream of corn.

7. Cook until heated through.

8. Season with salt and pepper.

Nutrition (per serving)

Calories 158 Carbs 24.2 g Fat 3.3 g Protein 8.5 g Sodium 919 mg

Stuffed Bell Peppers

Preparation time: 20 minutes

Cooking time: 30 minutes

Servings: 5

Ingredients:

- 6 large bell peppers, tops off, seeds removed
- 2 tablespoons vegetable oil
- 1 pound ground beef
- 2 cups white rice (cooked at home)
- ½ cups tomato sauce

Directions

1. Place the Dutch oven in the coals to heat.

2. Add the vegetable oil, beef, and cook until brown.

3. Add the tomato sauce and precooked rice, and mix well.

4. Spoon the filling into the cored bell peppers. Wipe out the oven with a paper towel.

5. Arrange the stuffed bell peppers in the Dutch oven, and cover. Place some coals on the lid.

6. Bake for 20 to 30 minutes until the peppers are tender.

7. Serve and enjoy.

Nutrition

Calories 480, total fat 10 g, Carb 66 g, Protein 30.5 g, sodium 306 mg

Sausage, Pepper & Potato Packets

Preparation time: 20 minutes

Cooking time: 25 minutes

Servings: 5

Ingredients:

- 3 red potatoes, cut in chunks
- 4 cooked dinner sausages, sliced
- 2 onions, sliced
- 2 tablespoons butter
- ½ teaspoon paprika

Directions

1. Mix all the ingredients in a large bowl.

2. Cut a long piece of heavy-duty foil into a 12x20 inch rectangle, and coat it with cooking spray.

3. Place the mixture in the center of the foil and enclose it to form a package.

4. Cook the packet a few inches above the coals on a grill rack, turning it twice.

5. After 25 minutes, check that the potatoes are cooked through. Serve!

Nutrition

Calories 434, total fat 22.5 g, Carb 30.3 g, Protein 24 g, sodium 688 mg

Preparation time: 10 minutes

Cooking time: 25 minutes

Servings: 5

Ingredients:

- 2 celery ribs, chopped
- 1-quart chicken broth
- ⅓ cup all-purpose flour
- 2 cups cooked chicken, cubed
- 1 (8¾-ounce) package precooked chicken-flavored rice

Directions

1. Add the oil to the Dutch oven and heat it over medium-high heat.
2. Add the vegetables and stir-cook until the carrots become soft, crisp, and tender.
3. Add the broth and flour to a mixing bowl. Mix well.
4. Pour the broth into the Dutch oven and bring to a boil, stirring occasionally.
5. Stir-cook for 5–6 minutes until thickened.
6. Add the other ingredients and cook over medium-low heat until cooked to satisfaction.
7. Serve warm.

Nutrition: Calories 224, Fat 7 g, carbs 23 g, Protein 15 g, sodium 741 mg

Creme Potato Chicken Soup

Preparation time: 10 minutes

Cooking time: 10 minutes

Servings: 5

Ingredients:

- 3½ cups water
- 4 cups shredded cooked chicken breast
- 2 (10¾-ounce) cans condensed cream of chicken soup, undiluted
- 1 pound frozen mixed vegetables, thawed
- 1 (14½-ounce) can potatoes, drained and diced

Directions

1. Add the water, chicken breast, chicken soup, vegetables, and potatoes to the Dutch oven. Bring to a boil.
2. Reduce heat to low, cover, and simmer for 8–10 minutes until the veggies are tender, stirring occasionally.
3. Mix in the cheese.
4. Serve warm with minced chives on top.

Nutrition

Calories 429, Fat 22 g, carbs 23 g, Protein 33 g, sodium 1464 mg

Dessert Recipes

Granola Over A Campfire

Preparation time: 10 minutes

Cooking time: 35 minutes

Servings: 4

Ingredients:

- ½ Cup Vegetable Oil
- 6 Cups Rolled Oats
- ½ to 1 Cup Maple Syrup
- 2 Cups Pecans or Almonds
- 1 cup Dried Cranberries

Directions:

1. Get your Dutch oven. Add your nuts and toss them around. It's a good idea to take the oven off the fire as you throw them around to ensure you do not burn them.

2. Once they begin to have a sweet smell of nutty, you can add the rolled oats. Cook this over the fire slowly until it transforms or becomes brown and nutty.

3. Take the oven off the heat and add the Vegetable oil and the Maple Syrup. You may add more or make it less syrup depending on the consistency you need.

4. Toss this together and put it in a bowl when it's ready. Add the dried Cranberries and eat warm. You can keep it covered also, and it will last for more Breakfasts to come.

Nutrition:

Calories 108, total fat 12.2 g, carb 37 g, Protein 8.1 g, sodium 146 mg

Wildberry Mascarpone Sliders

Preparation time: 15 minutes

Cooking time: 30 minutes

Servings: 4

Ingredients:

- 1 sheet puff pastry dough
- 2 cups fresh berry mixture, chopped
- ½ cup sugar
- ½ cup fresh basil chopped
- ½ cup mascarpone cheese

Directions

1. Lay the puff pastry dough out onto a flat surface. Using a cookie cutter or small glass, cut out circles approximately 1½" to 2" in diameter. Place on a cookie sheet and bake according to package instructions. Remove from oven and let cool.

2. In a bowl, combine the berries and sugar.

3. In another bowl, combine the basil and mascarpone cheese.

4. Spread the mascarpone mixture onto each puff pastry round. Top with a spoonful of berries.

5. Place on a serving platter and serve immediately.

Nutrition: Calories 458, total fat 21 g, carb 60 g, Protein 18.1 g, sodium 905 mg

Coconut Mandarin Cake

Preparation time: 10 minutes

Cooking time: 20 minutes

Servings: 3

Ingredients:

- ½ bag of shredded coconut
- 1 yellow or white cake mixed as directed
- 1 can drain mandarin oranges
- 1 cup brown sugar
- 1 stick of butter

Directions:

1. Place a parchment circle in a Dutch oven at the bottom of a 1-2. Spread the coconut out.

2. Place the mandarin oranges in any cute pattern on top of the coconut. Spread the top of the brown sugar.

3. Cut butter pats and put over brown sugar evenly. And scatter over the top of the mixed cake.

4. Put another ring on the lid (18-19) on a ring of coals (1 1-2). Cook for about 35-40 min until the cake is baked. Take off the heat. Clear the heat from the end. Let stand for 5 minutes or so. Then turn on a tray. Makes a minimum of 16 slices.

Nutrition: Calories 118, total fat 11 g, carb 65 g, Protein 18.1 g, sodium 155 mg

Preparation time: 15 minutes

Cooking time: 60 minutes

Servings: 8

Ingredients:

- 5 cups dark chocolate pieces
- 1 cup candied ginger, chopped into small pieces
- 1 cup pistachios, chopped

Directions

1. Line a baking sheet with parchment paper.
2. In a double boiler, melt the chocolate to a smooth consistency. Add in the ginger and stir well.
3. Spread the chocolate out in an even layer onto the parchment paper. Smooth with a spatula.
4. Sprinkle with chopped pistachios and allow to cool until hardened.
5. Break into small pieces before serving.

Nutrition:

Calories 145, total fat 43 g, carb 14 g, Protein 10.1 g, sodium 396 mg

Rich Brioche Pudding

Preparation time: 10 minutes

Cooking time: 50 minutes

Servings: 4

Ingredients:

- 5 cups day-old brioche, cubed
- 4 cups heavy cream
- 1 orange, juiced and zested
- 1½ cup brown sugar
- 9 eggs

Directions

1. Preheat oven to 375°F191°C.

2. Begin by cracking and separating the eggs. Leave three eggs whole and save only the yolks out of the remaining six. Whisk the whole eggs and the egg yolks together.

3. In a saucepan over medium heat, combine the heavy cream, ½ cup orange juice, 1 tablespoon orange zest, and brown sugar. Cook, stirring for 3-4 minutes.

4. Very slowly, incorporate the cream mixture into the eggs, whisking constantly to prevent cooking.

5. Place the brioche cubes in a large bowl and add the custard mixture. Toss to coat.

6. Transfer to a lightly oiled 9"x9" baking dish and place in the oven.

7. Bake for 40 minutes or until golden brown and hot, but still soft on the inside.

8. Serve warm or chilled.

Nutrition:

Calories 245, total fat 32 g, carb 57 g, Protein 10.1 g, sodium 126 mg

Preparation time: 10 minutes

Cooking time: 35 minutes

Servings: 3

Ingredients:

- 2 Cups Corn Bread Mix
- ½ Cup Water
- ½ Cup Canned Corn, Rinsed and Drained
- 2 Tablespoons Sugar
- ¼ Cup butter

Directions:

1. This delicious food is great for breakfast, lunch, dinner, or just a snack. Attach the mixture of cornbread and sugar and combine it in a pan. Then slowly add the water and continue to blend.

2. While you want daily mixing, you don't want to over-mix. Next, add the drained Canned Corn and add a different mix.

3. The trick to making Fritters is to make sure the Cooking Oil is superhot when we start. Start with your Dutch oven and add some oil to cover the bottom, it is likely to be about 1-fifth of Cooking Oil's quarter cup. Place some of the batters in the oil and cook until crispy at the bottom for about 3 minutes.

4. Then flip and also cook over for another 3 minutes. Drain them as the remainder of the batter is out on paper towels.

Nutrition:

Calories 238, total fat 23.2 g, carb 30 g, Protein 11 g, sodium 456mg

Preparation time: 10 minutes

Cooking time: 35 minutes

Servings: 3

Ingredients:

- 14 dinner rolls (let them thaw first),
- About ten pieces of cooked bacon (break them into little pieces)
- ¼ cup of melted butter
- Topping
- 2 cups of cheddar cheese, grated

Directions

1. Cut each dinner roll in half, and then roll them in the butter until they are well coated. Arrange the butter-coated rolls in the Dutch oven. Sprinkle the mixture with bacon and cheese.

2. Cover the lid and let the dough rise slowly. Set the temperature of the Dutch oven to 350 °F and bake the mixture for 30 minutes. You can now serve for breakfast or eat later during the day.

Nutrition:

Calories 431, total fat 19.2 g, carb 90 g, Protein 6 g, sodium 784 mg

Preparation time: 10 minutes

Cooking time: 30 minutes

Servings: 3

Ingredients:

- 8 oz. Barilla Fettuccine Noodles
- 1 1/4 cup Shredded Parmesan Cheese
- 1 cup Heavy Whipping Cream
- 1/2 cup butter 1 stick, sliced thinly
- 3 cups Swanson Chicken Broth

Directions;

1. Bring three cups of Chicken Broth to boil at Med / High heat in 5–6 quarters Dutch Oven.

2. Breakin half the fettuccine noodles and add to the boiling broth.

3. For 1-2 minutes, cook Fettuccine, stirring frequently.

4. Decrease the heat to medium and remove any Pot Chicken Broth waste. {I used a large spoon to remove the extra Broth immediately} Stir in cream, butter, and garlic powder and parmesan cheese.

5. Leave for 5 minutes continuously or until the cheese is completely melted.

6. Serve Immediately.

Nutrition: Calories 341, total fat 12 g, carb 34 g, Protein 16 g, sodium 184 mg

Chocolate Butterfinger Cake

Preparation Time: 10 minutes

Cooking Time: 30 minutes

Servings: 3

Ingredients:

- 1 chocolate cake mix
- 1 large Butterfinger candy bar broken in pieces
- 1 can sweeten condensed milk
- Nuts and ice cream
- 1 small jar Butterscotch topping

Directions:

1. Mix the cake according to the instructions and bake for 40 minutes or until the cake is finished at 350 ° or in a 1-2 Dutch oven.

2. Remove sweetened condensed milk and butterscotch over the cake when the cake is still dry. Sprinkle with the piece of chocolate. With nuts, ice cream, or whipped cream, serve warm.

Nutrition:

Calories 541, total fat 18 g, carb 81 g, Protein 12 g, sodium 123 mg

Preparation time: 10 minutes

Cooking time: 30 minutes

Servings: 3

Ingredients:

- 1 cup (2 sticks) butter
- 1 cup pecans; chopped
- 1 pkg. butter pecan cake mix
- 1/4 cup brown sugar
- 2 cans apple pie filling

Directions

1. In an 11-inch Dutch oven, proceed to dump 2 cans of apple filling.

2. Sprinkle the sugar on top and then add the cake mix and the pecans but do not stir.

3. Thinly slice the butter and spread it on top.

4. Bake at 350 for 45-60 minutes.

Nutrition:

Calories 221, total fat 32 g, carb 12 g, Protein 21 g, sodium 290 mg

Dutch Oven Brownie

Preparation time: 10 minutes

Cooking time: 50 minutes

Servings: 3

Ingredients:

- ½ cup canola or vegetable oil
- 3 tablespoons water
- 2 eggs
- 1 cup m&m baking bits (3/4 cup for batter + ¼ cup for topping)
- 18.3 oz. Betty crocker fudge brownie mix {1 box}

Directions

1. Preheat your oven to 325 degrees F.
2. Once done, lightly grease a 10-inch Dutch oven.
3. In a bowl, mix together the eggs, Brownie Mix, oil, water and 3/4 cup M&M Baking Bits.
4. Carefully spread the mixture into your Dutch oven.
5. Bake for 40 minutes. Once the time is up, remove from oven and evenly spread the remaining 1/4 cup of M&M Baking Bits on top.
6. Return to oven and bake for 10 minutes more or until done.

7. Once done, let the Dutch oven cool on the wire rack for some minutes and then use a plastic knife to slice the Brownie.

8. Serve and enjoy. You can serve with vanilla ice cream if you wish.

Nutrition:

Calories 234, total fat 10 g, carb 32 g, Protein 12 g, sodium 842 mg

Strawberry Cobbler

Preparation time: 10 minutes

Cooking time: 50 minutes

Servings: 3

Ingredients:

- 3 tablespoons butter, melted
- 1 stick butter {1/2 cup}, melted
- Philadelphia whipped cream cheese {8 oz.}
- 2 cans of strawberry pie filling {21 oz. Each}
- 1 box (15.25 oz.) Betty Crocker French vanilla cake mix

Directions

1. Preheat your oven to 350 degrees.

2. Place 1/2 stick of melted butter into the bottom of a 12-inch Dutch oven. Swirl the butter around to coat the Dutch oven evenly.

3. Once done, dump both cans of strawberry pie filling inside and use a wooden spoon to spread out evenly.

4. Spread dollops of cream cheese on top of the pie filling.

5. In a bowl, mix together the remaining 1 stick of melted butter and the Cake Mix. Use a spoon or your fingers to break up the chunks.

6. Spread the mixture on top of the cream cheese dollops and pie filling.

7. Bake for 50 minutes. The top should be crispy and the edges hot and bubbly.

8. Remove and serve with vanilla ice cream if you wish.

Nutrition:

Calories 214, total fat 23 g, carb 21 g, Protein 21 g, sodium 287 mg

Blueberry Dump Cake

Preparation time: 10 minutes

Cooking time: 40 minutes

Servings: 3

Ingredients:

- 1-pint blueberries

- 1/2 cup butter (1 stick or you could use margarine)

- 1 cup milk (you can use skim or you could use almond milk or other dairy free milk in place of regular milk)

- 1 cup sugar

- 1 cup flour (all-purpose or whole wheat pastry flour)

Directions

1. Preheat your oven to 375 and spray your Dutch oven with cooking spray or spread a bit of butter in it and set aside.

2. Melt the butter. You can melt it for 30 seconds in the microwave. In a bowl, combine the butter, flour, milk and sugar. Mix well and then pour into the prepared Dutch oven.

3. Spread the blueberries on top and then bake for 40-45 minutes. The edges should start to brown.

4. Remove from the oven and let it cool for 10 minutes.

5. Serve.

Nutrition: Calories 201, total fat 23 g, carb 12 g, Protein 13 g, sodium 732 mg

Preparation time: 10 minutes

Cooking time: 20 minutes

Servings: 3

Ingredients:

- ½ pack vanilla cake mix

- 1 cup lemon-lime soda (Sprite/7 Up)

- 4 cups fruit (peaches, apples, berries, etc.)

- 2 tablespoons unsalted butter, cold, diced

- Whipped cream

Directions

1. Lightly grease the Dutch oven with cooking spray.

2. Add the cake mix and soda to a mixing bowl. Mix well to make a thick batter.

3. Arrange the fruit in the Dutch oven; pour the batter over it.

4. Top with the diced butter and sugar.

5. Heat the Dutch oven to 350°F (175°C).

6. Cover and cook for 20 minutes until the top is golden brown and the juices are bubbling.

7. Serve warm with whipped cream.

Nutrition: Calories 282, Fat 6 g, carbs 57 g, Protein 3 g, sodium 304 mg

Cherry Clafouti

Preparation time: 10 minutes

Cooking time: 30 minutes

Servings: 3

Ingredients:

- ¾ pound fresh or frozen and thawed cherries stemmed and pitted
- 2 large eggs
- ¼ cup of sugar
- ½ cup whole milk
- 1 teaspoon vanilla extract
- ½ cup all-purpose flour

Directions

1. Preheat the Dutch oven to 400°F (200°C). Evenly spread butter to cover the inside surface.

2. Spread the cherries over the bottom.

3. Whisk the eggs in a bowl. Add the sugar. Mix until well blended and frothy.

4. Add the flour, milk, and vanilla to another mixing bowl. Mix well.

5. Combine the mixtures to make a smooth batter.

6. Pour the batter over the cherries.

7. Cook, uncovered, for 30 minutes until the top is golden brown. Check by inserting a toothpick; it should come out clean. If not, cook for a few more minutes.

8. Serve warm.

Nutrition

Calories 92, Fat 2 g, carbs 16 g, Protein 3 g, sodium 26 mg

Pecan Pralines

Preparation time: 10 minutes

Cooking time: 20 minutes

Servings: 3

Ingredients:

- 1 cup whipping cream
- 3 cups light brown sugar
- ¼ cup butter
- 2 tablespoons corn syrup
- 1 teaspoon vanilla extract

Directions

1. Preheat the Dutch oven to 350°F (175°C).

2. Spread the pecan halves in the Dutch oven and cook for 5 minutes. Stir-cook for another 5 minutes. Set aside.

3. Clean the Dutch oven and add the whipping cream, brown sugar, butter, and corn syrup.

4. Boil over high heat for 4–6 minutes until the sugar melts completely, stirring occasionally.

5. Remove from heat and add the pecans and vanilla; stir for 1–2 minutes. Let cool for a while.

6. Place a spoonful of the mixture on a wax paper; allow to firm up for 10–15 minutes.

7. Serve warm.

Nutrition

Calories 228, Fat 14 g, carbs 25 g, Protein 2 g, sodium 31 mg

Quick and Easy Pop Brownies

Preparation time: 10 minutes

Cooking time: 45 minutes

Servings: 3

Ingredients:

- 1 box brownie mix
- 1 can soda pop
- ¾ pound chocolate chips

Directions

1. Line the Dutch oven with parchment paper.

2. Add the brownie mix and soda to a mixing bowl. Mix well until you get a smooth mixture.

3. Pour the batter over the parchment paper. Sprinkle the chocolate chips on top.

4. Heat to 350°F (175°C) and bake for 45–60 minutes until well set. Check by inserting a toothpick; it should come out clean. If not, cook for a few more minutes.

5. Slice and serve warm.

Nutrition

Calories 241, Fat 13 g, carbs 35 g, Protein 2 g, sodium 16 mg

Chocolate Chip Cookies

Preparation time: 10 minutes

Cooking time: 30 minutes

Servings: 3

Ingredients:

- 1 cup butter, softened
- ¾ cup packed brown sugar
- 1 egg
- 1 teaspoon baking soda
- 2¼ cups flour

Directions

1. Add the butter-sugar to a mixing bowl. Mix well.

2. Beat the eggs in another bowl. Mix well.

3. Add the sea salt, baking soda, and flour; mix again.

4. Combine the mixtures until smooth.

5. Divide into 24 balls.

6. Line the Dutch oven with parchment paper and lightly grease it with cooking spray.

7. Arrange the balls on the bottom.

8. Cover and cook for 6 minutes. If cookies have turned light brown, take them out. If not, cook for 2–4 more minutes. Do not overcook.

9. Let cool for a while.

10. Serve warm.

Nutrition

Calories 220, Fat 11 g, carbs 29 g, Protein 2 g, sodium 100 mg

Dutch Oven Brownies

Preparation time: 10 minutes

Cooking time: 40 minutes

Servings: 3

Ingredients:

- 1 box brownie mix
- ½ cup melted butter
- 2 large eggs
- 1 cup of chocolate chips
- 1 teaspoon vanilla extract

Directions

1. Add the brownie mix to a large mixing bowl and stir in the melted butter, eggs, and water, and chocolate chips until just combined, being careful not to over-mix the batter.

2. Line the Dutch oven with a piece of parchment paper and pour in the brownie mixture.

3. Bake at 350°F (180°C) for 25–30 minutes.

4. Let the brownies cool slightly and then cut into squares and serve.

Nutrition

Calories 502, Fat 27 g, carbs 63.2 g, Protein 5.7 g, sodium 308 mg

Double Chocolate Cake

Preparation time: 10 minutes

Cooking time: 40 minutes

Servings: 3

Ingredients:

- 1 box chocolate cake mix
- ¼ cup whole milk
- 1 cup of chocolate chips
- 2 cups heavy whipping cream
- 3 tablespoons powdered sugar

Directions

1. Add the cake mix to a large mixing bowl and stir in the milk and chocolate chips until just combined, being careful not to over-mix the batter.

2. Line the Dutch oven with a piece of parchment paper and pour in the chocolate cake mixture.

3. Bake at 350°F (180°C) for about 30 minutes.

4. Remove the cake from the Dutch oven and place it on a cooling rack. Let it cool completely.

5. Add the whipping cream, powdered sugar, and vanilla extract to a large mixing bowl and beat with a hand mixer.

6. Cut the chocolate cake in half to create two layers. Spread half of the whipped cream on one layer, cover

with the second layer, and decorate the whole cake with whipped cream.

7. If desired, sprinkle with more chocolate chips for better presentation.

Nutrition

Calories 594, Fat 36.9 g, carbs 64.5 g, Protein 6.3 g, sodium 572 mg

Conclusion

When it comes to preparing food while camping, there are many things to consider. For example, some campers choose to bring their lighted gas stoves or grills while others just choose to use the same one that they used at home

Camping is an ideal way to enjoy fantastic local produce. The best food and drink for camping involves various things to different individuals (and differs widely based on whether you are camping in a vehicle or backpacking). Picnics and camping are generally a bit better, since if it's already done, you're only transporting it, but preparing a great meal. In contrast, camping is not that challenging, as long as you meet certain general instructions. Probably your home kitchen has a freezer, pantry, sufficient cabinets, and quick access to a nearby supermarket where thousands of choices are accessible for any meal. However, the camping kitchen of yours is a little more mounted down, perhaps limited to a cooler, storage box, plastic jar/container or two, and perhaps a weekend bag made of paper that remains in your car's backseat.

The natural wood smoke gives any dish an amazing taste, while the gentle crackle of flames enables campfire cooking a relaxing way to experience the great outdoors. However, you don't have to associate fewer ingredients on hand with dull recipes, especially when you realize how some main staples will blend in dozens of ways, if not hundreds, enabling you to cook up dishes to please a lonely hiker, a romantic couple, a starving family, as well as a whole crowd sitting across the campfire.

It is probably better to make all food planning you can do as minimal as possible while camping. Minimize the use of perishable food products and follow the proper sanitation precautions to ensure your group members' welfare. However, that picnic and cookouts are a feature of the camping culture. For this purpose, it is important to take care of all the precautions. There are a few food planning staples that you shouldn't skip, regardless of whether you intend to prepare for your upcoming camping trip or hiking. A case of matches and some fluid used as a firelighter are first and foremost.

The majority tend to cook over an outdoor fire at their campsite, so you'd be not so lucky without the need for a means to start one. For the dishes, a medium-sized to large-sized lightweight bowl, a similar size skillet, foil of aluminum, and a compact grill that can be put over a fire grate are the real necessities. This variation of cooking appliances helps produce Ham, eggs, lentils, and pasta. Finally, don't skip your spatula and tongs. It's far from enjoyable to pull food from a bare-handed fire.

Printed in Great Britain
by Amazon